秦兵馬俑

THE TERRACOTTA ARMY OF EMPEROR QIN SHI HUANG

中國旅遊出版社出版

PUBLISHED BY THE CHINA TRAVEL AND TOURISM PRESS

(京)新登字031號

圖書在版編目（CIP）數據

秦兵馬俑/袁仲一撰文；羅忠民，白亮攝影. - 2版. -
北京: 中國旅遊出版社，1996.5
ISBN 7-5032-0355-2

Ⅰ.秦... Ⅱ.①袁... ②羅... ③白... Ⅲ.陶俑，秦兵馬
俑－攝影集－中國 Ⅳ.K878.9-64

中國版本圖書館CIP數據核字（96）第05684號

秦 兵 馬 俑

中國旅遊出版社 編
中國旅遊出版社 出版
（北京建國門內大街甲九號）
撰 文: 袁仲一
攝 影: 羅忠民、白 亮
翻 譯: 朱景琪（英文）
編 輯: 李澤儒（中文）、董瑞成（美術）
　　　　白 亮（圖片）、孟憲玉（外文）
責任編輯: 白 亮
裝幀設計: 董 剛
印 刷: 北京利豐雅高長城印刷有限公司
發 行: 中國旅遊出版社
開 本: 大16 印張: 8.5 印數: 0001-3000
1996年5月第二版 第一次印刷
ISBN 7-5032-0355-2/J·25 （中英）
008500

文明史上的偉大奇觀
秦始皇陵兵馬俑

袁仲一

秦始皇陵兵馬俑坑,位於陝西省臨潼縣秦始皇陵東側1.5公里處,是秦始皇陵的一組大型陪葬坑。這組陪葬坑由三個兵馬俑坑組成。分別編爲一、二、三號。一號兵馬俑坑是1974年農民打井時偶然發現的,二號和三號兵馬俑坑是1976年秦俑考古隊通過鑽探發現的。三個兵馬俑坑的規模均很宏偉,總面積達二萬餘平方米;埋藏的文物豐富多彩,在已經發掘的試掘方內已出土木質戰車三十餘乘,和真人真馬大小相似的陶俑、陶馬兩千餘件,各種青銅兵器三萬餘件。根據已知情況推斷,三個兵馬俑坑內計有戰車百餘乘,陶馬六百餘匹,各類武士俑近七千件,以及大批的實用青銅兵器。

陶俑、陶馬的排列是按照古代軍陣編組置設的。一號兵馬俑坑約有陶俑、陶馬六千件,是以戰車與步兵組合排列的長方形軍陣;二號兵馬俑坑內約有陶俑、陶馬一千三百餘件,是戰車、騎兵、步兵混合編組的曲形軍陣;三號兵馬俑坑內有戰車一乘,陶馬四匹,陶俑六十八件,陶俑作儀衛式的夾道排列,是統帥一、二號兵馬俑坑軍隊的指揮部(古稱軍幕)。車馬和俑的製作,形象逼真,是秦國強大軍隊的縮影。對研究秦代的軍事裝備、編制和軍陣的編列等,提供了形象的實物資料。

秦俑的形象多彩多姿,塑造了多種具有一定性格特徵的人物形象。其風格渾厚、洗練,富有感人的藝術魅力,是中國古代雕塑藝術史上的一個奇峰,標誌着中國古代雕塑藝術至秦王朝時已臻於成熟,形成了民族的獨特風格。秦俑藝術在中國雕塑史上起着承前啟後的作用,具有劃時代的意義。

秦俑,這一古代文明史上偉大奇觀的發現,引起了中國和世界人們的矚目,被譽爲“世界的第八奇蹟”、“二十世紀最壯觀的考古發現”。包括兵馬俑坑在內的秦始皇陵園,已於1987年12月被聯合國教科文組織列入世界文化遺產清單,成爲世界人們古代精神文明的瑰寶。

一 秦始皇帝陵與兵馬俑坑

秦始皇是中國歷史上第一個統一的封建王朝的皇帝,是個曾對中國歷史的發展作出重大貢獻的杰出政治家。他生於公元前259年,公元前246年繼承王位,當時年僅13歲,國家的大事悉由大臣代理。22歲時實行加冕禮,開始親理朝政。他繼承先王的遺志,注意發展農業生產,獎勵軍功,使秦國很快富強起來。他運用秦國強大的兵力,經過一系列的戰爭,至公元前221年,先後消滅了韓、趙、魏、燕、楚、齊等六個封建割據的諸侯國,完成了統一中國的大業,建立了秦王朝。接着,又實行了一系列鞏固統一的措施,如統一文字、統一度量衡,統一法令,統一貨幣等等。這些措施,對中國後代社會的發展有着巨大的影響。

在統一全國後,秦始皇曾多次巡遊全國各地,視察民風,宣揚秦的文治武功。公元前210年,在最後的一次出巡途中,死於沙丘平臺(今河北省廣宗縣境內),同年九月葬於驪山北麓(今陝西省臨潼縣東),終年50歲。

秦始皇生前曾幻想長生不老,派遣徐福等一些方士到東海尋求長生不老的仙藥。方士玩弄的是一套騙術,仙藥當然不可能求

得。但另一方面秦始皇也深知人總是要死的這個自然規律,因而在他繼承王位後即開始修築陵墓,前後歷時37年。

秦始皇陵的規模很大,像一座高大的山丘。形狀爲截去尖部的四方錐體,陵墓封土底部近似方形,頂部廣闊平坦,中腰有兩個緩坡狀的階梯。原高五十丈(115米),陵基東西長485米,南北寬515米。因經兩千多年水土的流失,現存陵墓封土高76米,陵基部東西長345米,南北寬350米。封土下面就是地宮,地宮的四週環繞着用磚坯砌築的宮牆。宮牆的四面有門,正門在東邊。東邊五個門,其餘三面各有一門。地宮的中心部距現地表約30米,裏面放置秦始皇的棺槨及各種珍貴的陪葬物。根據《史記·秦始皇本紀》記載:秦始皇陵地宮像座宏偉的地下宮殿,各種“奇器珍怪”的東西陳設得滿滿的。地宮的頂部有日月星辰之象;下部“以水銀爲百川江河大海”;又“以人魚膏爲燭”,以使地宮內長期光明如晝。地宮內的各種珍異之物,爲防止有人盜掘,“令匠作機弩矢,有所穿近者輒射之”。上述記載的可信程度如何,由於始皇陵尚未經過考古發掘,還難以判斷。但是地宮中有大量的水銀存在,這一點已得到科學測試的驗證。1981年和1982年,中國地質科學院物探研究所經過兩次測試,發現始皇陵地宮的中心部位有強烈的汞(水銀)異常反應,其面積達12000平方米。說明地宮中“以水銀爲百川江河大海”的說法,大體是可信的。

經考古勘探發現,在秦始皇陵墓的週圍,地表原有呈南北向長方形的內外兩重城牆。內城牆南北長1355米,東西寬580米,週長3870米;外城牆南北長2165米,東西寬940米,週長6210米。城牆是用夯土築成,牆體大部分已經傾倒,僅存牆基,只有內城和外城的南牆還各有一段殘存於地表,殘高2-3米,牆基寬8米。內城和外城的四面有門。外城的四面各有一門,內城的東、西、南三面各有一門,北面二門。門上原來都有闕樓建築,內城的四隅並建有角樓。內城裏面原來還有寢殿、便殿等各種大型宮殿建築。因經火焚這些地面建築今已不存,僅在地面上堆積着大量的殘磚碎瓦及紅燒土遺蹟。

始皇陵週圍56.25平方公里的範圍內,歷年來不斷有各種重要的遺蹟、遺物發現。其中地下遺蹟、遺物分佈最密集的地方,是內外城垣以內及其附近,面積約2平方公里。目前已發現各種陪葬坑、陪葬墓及修陵工匠墓約近400座。整個始皇陵好像一座豐富的地下文物寶庫。其中比較重要的發現有兵馬俑坑、銅車馬坑、大型馬厩坑及93座小型馬厩坑,31座跽坐俑坑和珍禽異獸坑,45座陪葬墓,103座修陵工匠墓,以及各種各樣的府坑等等。

中國古代,人們有個傳統的觀念,認爲人死了以後像活着的人一樣,在另一個幽冥的世界裏生活。因此,對待死人要像活人一樣“事死如事生”。秦始皇生前是統治全國的至高無上的皇帝,死後也是如此。因而始皇陵園的建築佈局,是模擬其生前宮室的形狀。那高大陵墓的封土及封土下面的地宮,像是生前住的咸陽宮。那陵墓週圍的內外兩重城垣,像是京都的內城和外郭城。秦始皇生前出行時有大批的車馬儀仗,因而要製作銅車馬陪葬,以供其在幽冥的世界中使用。古代京城內都設有厩苑,厩苑內飼養着專供宮廷使用的大批駿馬,所以秦始皇陵園內也就有象徵宮廷厩苑的大型和小型馬厩坑。始皇陵園內的珍禽異獸坑,是象徵宮廷的苑囿,苑囿內有

各種珍禽異獸，以供始皇遊獵觀賞。兵馬俑坑內的大批戰車、騎兵和步兵羣，是象徵守衛京城的部隊。綜上所述，秦始皇把生前的一切都模擬於地下，地下王國是地上王國的再現。

上面就秦始皇陵園的建築佈局及其設計意圖作了扼要的介紹。由此可知，兵馬俑坑的出現並不是偶然的，它是陵園建築的一個有機組成部分。秦始皇生前用強大的軍隊統一了中國，他深知軍隊的重要性，所以他把軍隊的形象模擬於地下，用以守衛亡靈。

二　兵馬俑坑的發現

秦始皇陵兵馬俑坑，位於秦始皇陵東側的西楊村南。這裏原是一片樹林，地面上覆蓋着砂石，墓塚纍纍，夜晚經常有野獸出没。如此荒涼的原野，誰也没有想到地下竟埋藏着人類文明史上的偉大奇觀——八千兵馬俑。1974年3月，臨潼縣晏寨鄉西楊村的農民楊志發、楊鵬躍、楊步治等人在村南打井。當挖到2米深時，發現了紅燒土硬塊；挖到4.5米深時，發現了陶俑殘片和青銅兵器弩機、箭頭，以及磚鋪的地面。他們感到奇怪，就把工程停下，向臨潼縣文化館彙報。文化館立即派人到現場考察，并收集了已出土的文物。接着，陝西省及國家文物事業管理局的領導和考古學專家又考察了現場，並委託陝西省組織考古隊進行勘探和發掘。筆者有幸作爲考古隊的一員首先進駐了秦俑考古工地。當時，我們根據一般的考古經驗，認爲俑坑的規模不會太大，大約10－15天的時間可以挖完。事實完全出乎想象之外。經過6個月的勘探和試掘，發一號兵馬俑坑東西長230米，南北寬62米，距現地面深4.5－6.5米，佔地面積14260平方米，裏面埋藏着高大的陶俑、陶馬約六千件。這樣規模巨大、數量衆多的兵馬俑坑，我們從事了幾十年考古工作的人員還從來没有碰到過，在中國和世界考古史上也從來没有發現過。大家欣喜若狂，高興的心情難以用筆墨形容。

國家對這一巨大的發現非常重視。爲了保護好這個珍貴的文化遺產，1975年決定撥巨款在一號兵馬俑坑上建造遺址展覽大廳，把一號兵馬俑坑全部罩住，以防風雨侵蝕，另外也便於人們參觀。1976年基建工程也正式開始。我們考古人員隨之轉入對一號兵馬俑坑週圍地區的勘探，希望能够再找到幾個兵馬俑坑。1976年夏天，在一號兵馬俑坑的東端北側相距20米的地方，又發現了二號兵馬俑坑。其平面呈曲尺形，東西長124米，南北寬98米(包括門道)，距現地表深約5米，面積約6000平方米。經過試掘獲知，二號兵馬俑坑內埋藏着木質戰車八十九乘，拉車的陶馬和騎兵的陶質鞍馬四百七十餘匹，各類大型武士俑九百餘件，總共有陶俑、陶馬一千三百餘件。

繼二號兵馬俑坑發現之後不久，我們在一號兵馬俑坑的西端北側，又鑽探出三號兵馬俑坑。兩坑相距25米，東距二號兵馬俑坑約120米。三號兵馬俑坑的平面呈"凹"字形，東西長17.6米，南北寬21.4米，距現地表深5.2－5.4米，面積376.64平方米。裏面有木質戰車一乘，陶俑、陶馬72件。

在一號兵馬俑坑的中部北側約20米處，我們還鑽探出一個未建成的兵馬俑坑。坑的平面呈橫長方形，東西長48米，南北寬96米，距現地表深4.8米，面積4608平方米。坑內積滿了淤泥和砂石，没有發現陶俑、陶馬以及其它遺蹟、遺物。這是由於秦王朝末年農民大起義，修築始皇陵和兵馬俑坑的工人被調去打仗，而被迫停建的。因爲這個坑內没有陶俑、陶馬，人們計算兵馬俑坑時未把它列在內，只説有三個兵馬俑坑。

一號兵馬俑坑遺址展覽大廳的基建工程於1978年5月竣工。我們隨即開始了對一號兵馬俑坑的正式發掘。現已發掘2000平方米，出土木質戰車八乘，陶俑、陶馬約千餘件，各種青銅兵器三萬餘件。目前發掘工作仍在進行中。三號兵馬俑坑上的展覽大廳於1988年12月建成，1989年對三號兵馬俑坑開始發掘和進行復原陳列。二號

兵馬俑坑遺址展覽大廳的基本建設工程，已於1990年竣工；接着對二號坑進行正式發掘。待一、二、三號兵馬俑坑的發掘工作全部完成，那一列列、一行行排列有序的八千兵馬俑，將以它恢宏的氣勢展現在人們的面前，再現秦軍兵強馬壯叱吒風雲的英姿。

許多觀衆看了兵馬俑坑後，往往提出這樣的疑問：如此龐大的兵馬俑羣，歷史上是否有所記載？關於秦始皇陵墓的情況，《史記》、《漢書》等許多古文獻上都記載得比較清楚，而關於兵馬俑坑卻史無明文。只是《漢舊儀》上提到過這樣一件事，秦始皇使丞相李斯主持修建陵墓。當陵墓的主體工程修得差不多要竣工時，李斯向秦始皇匯報説："臣斯所將徒隸七十二萬人，治驪山者(即修始皇陵)，已深已極，鑿之不入，燒之不然，叩之空空如下天狀"。意思是説陵墓已挖得很深很大，內部佈置得如天下人間之狀。言下之意是想説可以結束了吧？始皇聽着下令説："其旁行三百丈，乃止"。經實測，兵馬俑坑大約在這個範圍之內，可能就是這次定下來的擴建工程之一。另外，唐代人蘇頲的《鼂上記》記述一件趣聞："都方回葬婦於驪山，治墓多乎夷占墳。後壞一塚，構制甚偉，器物殊盛，塚發聞鼓角聲"。所壞古塚的形制如何，言之不詳。但根據其規模巨大，埋藏的器物衆多，"塚發聞鼓角聲"等情況分析，有可能是發現了兵馬俑坑後的誇張説法。至今當地羣衆還有類似的傳説。

我們在對兵馬俑坑勘探和發掘的過程中也發現，在1974年以前就有一些人見到過兵馬俑。在二號兵馬俑坑的上面曾發現東漢初期(公元一世紀前期)的一座古墓。墓穴正好挖在一組騎兵的陶馬、陶俑身上。陶俑、陶馬被打破和搬動。説明遠在一千八百多年前已有人發現了地下埋藏的兵馬俑。這是目前所知兵馬俑的最早發現者。自十七世紀末期以來，這裏已是當地羣衆的墓地，僅在一號兵馬俑坑上就發現了十餘座墓葬，墓穴都挖及到了陶俑上。我們在考古調查的過程中，也遇到當地的老百姓説，他們的祖先在挖墓時曾看到過叫不出名字的怪物——陶俑。一位七十多歲的和萬春老人曾講道：他十歲左右的時候，父親在地裏打井，在井壁上見到一個跟人一樣高大的怪物。本來井底已見了水，不幾天井水突然枯竭。現在想來，可能是地下有縫隙，漏水了。可是當時他父親卻認爲是怪物興妖作怪，於是把它吊上來，放在太陽地裏曬。結果還是不見水，就吊在樹上把它打碎了。這説明在歷史上曾先後斷斷續續地有人發現過埋在地下的兵馬俑，由於不知道它是何物，或認爲它是不祥之物，所以没有引起世人的重視。兵馬俑坑離現在的地表，一般是5米左右，並不很深。隨着農田水利建設的發展，以及人們對保護文物知識的增多，應該説它的發現在今天是必然的，只是時間的早晚罷了。

三　兵馬俑坑的建築結構

一、二、三號兵馬俑坑，是一組佔地面積達20780平方米的宏偉的地下建築羣。目前觀衆看到的兵馬俑展覽大廳，是最早發現的一號兵馬俑坑。其平面呈東西向的長方形。坑的四面各有五個斜坡形門道。南、北兩側的門道較小(長12米，寬1.6－4.8米)，是偏門。東西兩端的門道較大(長15－20米，寬3.8－6.6米)，是主要門道。根據陶俑、陶馬都面東排列，可知一號兵馬俑是坐西面東，正門在東邊。進門後，坑的東西兩端各有一條南北長60米，寬3.45米的長廊；坑的南北兩側各有一條長約180米，寬約2米的邊廊。在四面環廊之間有九條東西向的過洞，每條過洞長約180米，寬約3.5米。過洞與過洞之間以夯土牆相隔。坑的底部以青磚墁鋪，坑的頂部搭蓋棚木及覆蓋黃土，形成坑道式的土木結構的地下大型建築。其具體構築方法是：先在平地上挖一長方形的土壙；在土壙內築起一道道的東西向的夯土隔牆；在隔牆的南北兩側及坑的四週邊壁，每隔1.4－1.76米立一根木柱；木柱的上端承托着枋木；在枋木和夯土隔牆上一根挨一根地排着棚木；棚木上再覆蓋蓆子、紅膠泥土和黃土，從而構成

坑頂。坑頂高出當時的地表約2米,遠遠看去是個長方形的土臺,土臺上再沒有其它磚瓦木構建築。從坑底到坑頂的內部空間高3.2米。坑的四面有門。把陶俑、陶馬由門道放進坑內後,即把門用立木封堵,門道用夯土填實。這樣就形成了一座封閉式的地下軍事營壘。在這個營壘四週的邊廊內排列的是步兵俑,過洞內是戰車和步兵俑相間排列。

二號兵馬俑坑的平面呈曲尺形,其東端、西端和北側,各有斜坡形門道四條、五條和二條,坐西面東,正門在東邊。二號俑坑的結構比較複雜,平面大體可劃分爲四個單元。第一單元,位於俑坑的東端,即曲尺形的頂部。它四面環有長廊,中間有四條東西向的過洞,過洞與過洞之間以夯土牆相隔。此單元內放置的都是手持弓弩的步兵俑,也就是説它是弩兵的營壘。第二單元,位於俑坑的右側,即曲尺形的南半部。其東西兩端各有一條南北向的長廊,中部有八條東西向的過洞。過洞與過洞之間亦以夯土牆相隔。此部分排列的全是戰車,是車陣的營壘。第三單元,位於曲尺形的中部。其東端和第一單元相接,左右兩側和二、四單元相鄰,西端突出於曲尺形之後形成一個"小斗子"。有兩條東西向的夯土隔牆,把此單元分隔成三條東西向的過洞。過洞內由東而西依次是戰車和步兵俑相間排列,最後的"小斗子"部分排列的是騎兵俑。這裏是戰車、步兵、騎兵組成的長方形的營壘。第四單元,位於俑坑的左側,即曲尺形的北半部。東端和第一單元之間以夯土牆相隔,牆上有門,以資相通。此單元亦有兩條東西向的夯土隔牆,把其分隔成三條東西向的過洞。過洞內排列着騎兵俑,是騎兵的營壘。以上四個單元相對來説是各自獨立的,合起來成爲一個嚴密的整體。二號兵馬俑坑的構築方法,與一號兵馬俑坑相同,亦是在平地上先挖成一個曲尺形的土壙,在土壙內築起一條條的夯土隔牆。在隔牆的兩側及坑的四週邊壁排列着木柱,柱上承托枋木,在枋木和上隔牆上密集地搭蓋着棚木,棚木上覆蓋一層席子,再覆蓋黃土。坑的底部用磚墁鋪。俑坑內部的空間高度3.2米。從門道內把陶俑、陶馬放進坑內後,即把門用立木封堵,門道內用夯土填實。從而形成一座封閉式的曲尺狀的地下軍事營壘。

三號兵馬俑坑的平面呈"凹"字形,坐西面東,東邊有一個斜坡形的門道。進門後迎面就是一個車馬房,內放駟馬戰車一乘。由此向右拐有一南北向長廊,長廊內有兩列武士俑相向而立,作夾道式排列。在此長廊的西側有一東西向長方形的大廳。大廳的南北兩側夾道排列着武士俑,地面上發現有鹿角和動物骨骼等遺物。古代打仗之前首先要進行祭祀,祈求神靈保佑,並進行鼓動性的誓師,稱之爲"禱戰"。從發現的鹿角和獸骨分析,這裏可能是"禱戰"的地方。由中間的車馬房往左拐,亦有一南北向的長廊。長廊內有兩列武士俑相向而立,作夾道式排列。長廊的中部西側連接着一東西向的過道。沿着過道進去是一前廳,過了前廳就進入了後室。在過道和前廳、後室內,都有擔任警衛的武士俑作夾道式的排列。根據前廳和後室的佈局情況分析,前廳似爲將帥接見軍吏和辦理軍務之處,後室是就寢處。三號兵馬俑坑的構築方法與一、二號兵馬俑坑相同,亦是土木結構的地下坑道式的建築,其內部空間高3.6米。陶俑、陶馬放進坑內後,即把門用立木封堵,門道用夯土填實。

一、二、三號兵馬俑坑和未建成的俑坑,是緊密相連的一組地下建築。一號坑是右軍的營壘,二號坑是左軍的營壘,未建成的坑是原來打算建築的中軍的營壘,三號坑是個指揮部,從而構成一組龐大的地下營壘。古代駐紮軍的"營壘"又稱爲"壁壘",出土殘簡上稱作"壁"。例如秦、趙的長平大戰,秦軍和趙軍的壁壘相對。秦軍數次挑戰,趙將廉頗堅壁不出。秦軍求戰不得,利用離間計,說廉頗並不可怕,可怕的是趙括。趙王信以爲真,用趙括代替廉頗爲主帥。秦軍又挑戰,趙括率軍出壁追擊。秦軍用奇兵插入趙軍壁壘之間,斷其後路,終於殲滅趙軍四十餘萬人。又《尉繚子》記載,壁壘內部各軍都有一定的界域,不能互相越界,人員不能隨意走動,違者處斬。

秦俑坑的建築結構也是如此,各軍的界域分明,氣氛肅穆。

一號兵馬俑坑因經過火焚塌陷;二號兵馬俑坑的局部經火焚塌陷,其餘部分因棚木腐朽自然塌陷;三號兵馬俑坑未經火焚係因棚木朽毀塌陷,但在塌陷前,曾進去過人,陶俑、陶馬被打碎。一號兵馬俑坑在被焚塌陷前也曾遭到人爲的破壞,兵器被拿走很多,有的陶俑、陶馬被打得粉碎。俑坑究竟是被什麼人燒的,目前還找不到確實的證據。不過根據文獻記載,公元前207年項羽入關曾"燔其宮室營宇"。秦咸陽宮、阿房宮及始皇陵的地面建築都被燒毀,俑坑亦可能是同時被項羽的軍隊燒的。這僅是一種推斷,確切的被焚原因尚待進一步探究。

四　兵馬俑的分類和隊形編列

秦是一個軍事大國,擁有戰車千乘,騎萬匹,步兵百餘萬。秦始皇憑藉着強大的軍力,先後消滅了其它六個諸侯割據的國家,完成了統一中國的大業,建立了秦王朝。秦國軍隊的兵種,據史書記載有戰車、騎兵、步兵和水軍。前三種兵種主要用於中原和北方地區作戰,水軍主要用於江河較多的南方地區作戰。關於秦國各兵種的情況,歷史文獻記載得比較簡略。各兵種的服裝、武器裝備、戰鬥隊形的編組等問題,長期以來人們都沒有得到一個鮮明的認識。秦始皇陵兵馬俑坑的發現,爲解決這些問題提供了具體的實物例證。兵馬俑坑除無水軍外,其餘三種兵種都有,而且人數衆多,內容豐富多彩,形象生動逼真,是秦國軍隊的縮影。

(一)　戰車、騎兵和步兵俑的類別

1.　戰車

秦始皇陵兵馬俑坑出土的戰車都是木車,車的大小和真車一樣。根據出土車的遺蹟觀察,所有的戰車都是雙輪、單轅。轅長3.7—3.96米。轅的前段揚起,後段平直壓於車輿下。車輿(即車廂)呈橫長方形,寬約1.4米,前後長約1.2米。輿的四週圍有高約40厘米呈欄格狀的圍欄,後面設門以備上下車用。車輪高1.35米。車轅的前端縛一橫木,古名爲衡,衡上縛有雙軛,用以駕馬。車前駕有陶馬四匹。陶馬的大小和真馬相似,身長約2米,通首高1.72米。車通體髹漆,有的並繪有精緻的圖案花紋。陶馬通體塗棗紅色,黑鬃、黑尾、白蹄甲。車馬上的駕具齊備,與實用的戰車沒有大的差異。

秦始皇陵兵馬俑坑出土的戰車,根據車上的乘員數和裝飾的不同,可分爲指揮車、副車、駟乘車和一般戰車等四種類型。

①指揮車

指揮車與一般戰車的主要區別,是車的裝飾比較華麗,通體塗黑漆,繪有精美的幾何形圖案花紋,車上有圓形華蓋,並懸有鐘、鼓。車上有陶俑三件:一爲將軍俑,二爲御手俑,三爲車右俑。三件俑在車後作橫一字形排列。一般是御手俑居中,其職責是負責駕御車馬;將軍俑居左,其職責是掌握車上的鐘、鼓,指揮軍隊的進退;車右俑居於右側,手持兵器,其職責是負責作戰,以保護車上的指揮官,當遇到障礙時負責推車。

車上三件俑的裝束、姿態各不相同。將軍俑身穿紅色中衣,外罩紫色或綠色外衣,披彩色魚鱗甲,足穿齊頭翹尖履,頭戴鶡冠,身佩長劍,昂首挺胸立於車上,神態異常威武。御手俑身穿綠色長衣,外套赭黑色鎧甲,脛著護腿,足穿履,頭戴長冠,雙臂前舉,雙手半握拳作用力牽拉馬轡狀。車右俑身穿紅色或綠色長衣,脛著護腿,身披鎧甲,頭戴長冠,左手作按劍狀,右臂前曲作持戈、矛等長兵器狀。

指揮車上懸置鐘、鼓。鐘係青銅鑄造,通高27厘米,上有精緻的變相夔鳳紋。鼓爲扁圓形,面徑約50厘米,高約20厘米,鼓壁上有等距離的三個銅環以便懸掛。中國古代作戰是用金鼓鈴旗指揮。古兵書《尉繚子》說:"鼓之則進,重鼓則擊;金之則止,重金則退;鈴傳

3

令也;旗麾之左則左,麾之右則右……鼓失次者有誅,讙譁者有誅,不聽金鼓鈴旗而動者有誅"。

②副車(又名佐車)

兵馬俑坑出土的副車的形制與指揮車相同,但車上沒有華蓋和鐘鼓。一般車上都有乘員三人,副車上只有乘員二人,一為御手,一為車右。御手居於車之正中,車右居於車之右側,左邊缺少一人。左邊是尊者之位,尊者不在車上古代叫作"曠左",又名"虛左"。古代作戰時,將領公乘的車叫主車。在主車之後一般都有副車跟隨。《禮記·檀弓》記載着這樣一個故事:魯莊公率兵與宋人戰於乘丘,馬驚敗績,莊公從主車上墜下,後邊跟隨的副車"授綏"(綏是上車時攀拉用的帶子)。莊公攀綏登上了副車,免於被俘。兵馬俑坑出土的副車見於二號俑坑騎兵陣的陣首,當為騎兵統帥的副車。

③馹乘車

二號和三號兵馬俑坑各出土馹乘車一輛。如三號兵馬俑坑出土的馹乘車,車的形制與指揮車相同,車上亦有華蓋,但未發現鐘、鼓。車上有陶俑四件:一為御手俑,一為軍吏俑,其餘兩件為甲士俑。御手俑的裝束、姿態與指揮車上御手俑相同。軍吏俑身穿紅色長衣,外披帶彩色花邊的護胸甲,脛著護腿,足登履,頭戴長冠,左手作按劍狀,右手半握拳,持物不明。其餘兩名甲士俑的服飾相同,都着長衣,披鎧甲,脛著護腿,足穿履,頭戴長冠,手作持兵器狀。

古代戰車上一般只有乘員三人,有乘員四人者十分罕見。此種乘法不是通例,因為增加一人會影響戰車的速度,同時因車上人員擁擠不利於甲士揮戈與敵格鬥。從二號和三號兵馬俑坑馹乘車出土的位置分析,都位於隊列的最前端,似為前驅車,又名先驅車,行軍時導行在先,作戰時"挑戰前驅",即在戰前向敵軍致戰,表示必戰的決心,然後兩軍交鋒。

④一般戰車

一般戰車,即戰士所乘的車,車亦為雙輪,單轅,前駕四馬。車上沒有華蓋和鐘、鼓。有乘員三人:一名御手、兩名甲士。御手居於車之正中,負責駕御車馬;兩名甲士分列於御手的左右,負責作戰。

二號兵馬俑坑出土的一般車上的御手俑和甲士俑的裝束和姿態,都較別致。御手俑所穿的鎧甲除把上半身罩於甲內外,並把雙臂全部罩住,手上並有護手甲,頸部有盆領(即頸甲),脛部著護腿,頭罩巾幘,幘外再戴長冠。這種裝束為重裝備。古代戰車都是立乘,御手立在車上駕御車馬,目標較大,所以其防護裝備要好,以免受敵箭射傷使車馬失去控馭,而致敗績。兩名甲士的服飾相同,姿態各異。都是身穿上衣,外披鎧甲,脛著護腿,足穿履,頭戴赤色介幘。右邊的甲士左足向前作稍息式立姿,左臂衣袖綰於肘部,伸掌作用力按車貌;右臂前曲作持長兵器狀,頭微向上側轉仰視前方。左側的甲士其動態恰與之相反,形成對稱。兩者目光相交,英姿勃勃,極為生動傳神。

戰車上的御手要經過嚴格訓練。秦的法律規定,學習駕車,經過四年仍不會駕馭者,罰負責教練的人一盾,本人免職,並補服四年內應服的徭役(見秦簡《秦律雜抄》)。戰車上的甲士也要經過選拔,選拔的標準:"取年四十已下,長七尺五寸(1.73米),走能逐奔馬,及馳而乘之,前後左右上下周旋,能縛束旌旗,力能彀八石弩射前後左右,皆便習者,名曰武車之士"(《六韜·武車士》)。秦俑中的車士個個身材雄健,高達1.8米以上,顯然是這種經過選練的車士形象。

2. 騎兵俑

騎兵俑都出土於二號兵馬俑坑內,四匹陶馬一組,三組一列,九列(108匹馬)組成一個長方形的騎兵陣。陶馬的大小和真馬相似,身長約2米,通首高1.72米。馬剪鬃、辮尾,背上雕着馬鞍,鞍面有一行行的鞍釘,並塗有紅、白、藍、赭四彩。鞍的質地似為皮革。鞍下墊韉,韉的四週綴有流蘇及彩色條帶。鞍的後部有鞦澤繞於馬的臀部。鞍的兩側有條肚帶把鞍固着於馬背上。馬頭部套有絡頭(俗稱籠頭)、銜、鑣以及馬繮。銜、鑣係銅質,絡頭和馬繮係用銅絲串聯青石管組成。每匹馬前立有騎士俑一件。騎士俑的頭戴圓形小帽,身穿窄袖齊膝長衣,外披短甲(甲長僅及腰部),腰束革帶,足登靴。作一手牽拉馬繮,一手提弓貌。

秦國的法律規定:騎兵用的馬和騎士要經過嚴格的挑選。挑選的標準是:馬高五尺八寸(1.33米)以上,馬的奔馳羈繫要聽從指揮。騎士自從軍人員中挑選。到軍後進行考核,如馬被評為下等,負責選送馬的縣令、縣丞罰二甲,司馬罰二甲,並革職永不叙用(《秦律雜抄》)。騎士選拔的標準,《六韜·武騎士》記載:"選騎士之法,取年四十已下,七尺五寸(1.73米)已上,壯健捷疾,超絕倫等,能馳騎彀射前後左右,週旋進退,越溝塹,登丘陵,冒險阻,絕大澤,馳強敵,亂大眾者,名曰武騎之士。"秦俑坑出土的騎兵陶馬通首高1.72米,至馬鬐甲(肩部)高1.33米。古今測量馬的高度不能以馬頭的高為準,因馬頭高低不易確定,而必須以馬鬐甲的高度為準。秦俑坑出土的騎兵陶馬的高度,與秦國法律規定的騎兵馬的高度完全相符。秦俑坑出土的騎士俑身高都在1.8米以上,身材勻稱,神態機敏,壯健輕捷,是經過選練的騎士的典型形象。這對於我們研究秦國的騎兵史,是一批珍貴的形象資料。

3. 步兵俑

秦俑坑出土的步兵俑數量最多。以職位的高低分,可分為軍吏俑和一般士兵俑兩大類。而每一大類中又可分為若干小類。

①軍吏俑

軍吏俑中又有將軍俑、中級軍吏俑和下級軍吏俑的區別。其區別的主要標誌,是鎧甲和冠的不同。將軍俑大都穿彩色魚鱗甲,頭戴鶡冠,足登方口齊頭翹尖履,雙手交垂於腹前作拄劍狀,昂首挺立,面容嚴肅,神態威武。

中級軍吏俑有兩種不同的裝束,一為身穿胡服,着齊邊甲,戴雙版長冠。如一號兵馬俑坑四、八、十過洞出土的三件中級軍吏俑,都是身穿窄袖胡服,外披前後擺平齊的鎧甲,脛著護腿,足登履,頭戴雙版長冠,手作握兵器狀,肅然佇立。再如一號兵馬俑坑二過洞和二號兵馬俑坑第四試掘方出土的中級軍吏俑,身穿交領右衽長衣(漢服),其鎧甲僅有護胸甲而無背甲,以十字相交的兩條背帶繫結,背帶上有精緻的圖案花紋。下身着長褲,足登方口齊頭翹尖履,頭戴雙版長冠,一手作按劍狀,一手半握拳,持物不明。二號兵馬俑坑第四試掘方出土的中級軍吏俑立於將軍俑的身旁,神態恭謹,顯係將軍俑的副手,其地位低於將軍俑。

下級軍吏俑出土的數量較多,依其裝束的不同可分兩種:一種是不穿鎧甲的輕裝下級軍吏俑;一是身穿鎧甲的重裝下級軍吏俑。下級軍吏俑與一般士兵俑的主要區別:下級軍吏俑頭戴長冠,一般士兵俑不戴冠;再者,一般士兵的鎧甲的甲片較大而甲片的數量少,下級軍吏俑的鎧甲甲片小,但甲片的數量多。下級軍吏俑與中級軍吏俑的主要區別是:中級軍吏俑頭戴雙版長冠,下級軍吏俑頭戴單版長冠;中級軍吏俑的鎧甲都有彩色的邊緣,而下級軍吏俑的鎧甲沒有彩繪的圖案花紋。如一號兵馬俑坑東南角出土的一件輕裝的下級軍吏俑,身穿齊膝長衣,腰間束帶,下着短褲,腿紮行縢(裹腿),足登雙口齊頭翹尖履,頭戴單版長冠。左手作按劍狀,右手作持戈,矛等長兵器狀。挺胸昂首,神態勇武。身穿鎧甲的下級軍吏俑,身穿長衣,外披鎧甲,腿部有的紮行縢,有的著護腿,足上有的穿履,有的穿靴。手裏的提弓,有的持戈、矛等長兵器。個個身材壯健,神態勇武。

②士兵俑

秦俑坑出土的士兵俑以其裝束的不同,可分為不穿鎧甲的輕裝士兵俑和穿鎧甲的重裝士兵俑兩種。輕裝士兵俑身穿長度及膝的上衣,腰束革帶,下着短褲,腿紮行縢,頭綰圓形髮髻,足穿履,手提弓弩或持戈、矛、戟等長兵器。其裝束輕便,行動輕捷,故名輕裝士兵俑。輕裝士兵俑多位於軍陣的前鋒部位。如一號兵馬俑坑的前鋒部隊有204件步兵俑,其中穿鎧甲的俑只有3件,其餘均為不穿鎧甲的輕裝步兵俑。因爲前鋒部隊要求行動要迅速，能出敵不意，乘敵不備地迅疾打擊敵軍，所以其裝束一定要輕便。這説明遠在兩千多年以前的軍事家，已經懂得防護裝備與打擊敵人的辯證關係。也就是説防護裝備是爲了保護自己，消滅敵人，但消滅敵人是目的。在一定情況下，爲了消滅敵人就要輕裝。消滅敵人是第一位，防護裝備處於第二位，後者要服從於前者。

身穿鎧甲的重裝士兵俑，其主要特徵是身穿長度及膝的上衣，外披鎧甲，下着短褲，腿紮行縢或縛護腿，足上有的穿履，有的穿靴。手中有的提弓弩，有的持戈、矛、戟等長兵器。重裝士兵俑的頭上有的綰着圓形的髮髻，有的腦後結綰六股寬辮形的扁髻，有的頭戴赤色巾幘(即圓椎形的軟帽)。目前在兵馬俑坑内還没有發現戴頭盔的步兵俑。從歷史文獻記載看，秦國軍隊是有頭盔的，但打仗的時候秦國的軍隊非常勇敢，往往免盔而戰，以顯示其勇敢不怕死的氣概。秦俑坑出土的步兵俑不戴頭盔，當是這種大無畏精神的體現。

(二) 戰車、騎兵、步兵俑的排列

古代軍隊作戰的時候要排成一定的隊形，即所謂軍陣，也就是戰鬥隊形的編組。軍隊只有編列成一定的戰鬥隊形，才有戰鬥力。《六韜·均兵》説，如果單兵作戰，"一騎不能當步卒一人"；當列成戰鬥隊形時，"一騎當步卒八人"。恩格斯也曾説過："非正規騎兵隊形散亂，衝鋒時互不協調和没有嚴整的陣列，因此絲毫也不能動摇密集的、勇猛行進的隊形。只有當正規騎兵的戰術隊形陷入混亂和開始單騎戰鬥時，非正規的優越性才能顯示出來"(《馬克思恩格斯全集》第十四卷320頁)。軍隊不同於武術隊，個人的技藝處於第二位，軍陣處於第一位。所以古代的軍隊無論是野戰還是攻城或追擊敵兵，都要始終保持一定的隊形，"勇者不得獨進，怯者不得獨退"(《孫子兵法·軍爭》)。有敢擅自離開隊形的要受軍法懲處。周武王伐紂，曾命令兵卒每前進幾步刺殺幾下，就要回顧編列，要始終保持整齊的戰鬥隊形。歷史上由於戰鬥隊形是否整齊而導到戰爭勝敗的事例很多。如春秋時鄢陵之戰，楚軍由於"陣而不整"遭到慘敗。泌之戰，晉軍在敗局已成的情況下，而晉的上軍由於保持了隊形得以順利撤退，晉的其餘軍則因隊列散亂而覆滅。所以自古以來歷代的軍事家對軍陣的編列都十分重視。可惜由於資料的缺乏，人們對古代的陣形已成了難解之謎。秦始皇兵馬俑軍陣是一幅生動的古代陣形的圖譜，對於我們了解古代的陣形提供了實物例證。

1、一號兵馬俑坑軍陣

一號俑坑約有兵馬俑六千餘件，目前揭示出來的僅有武士俑千餘件、戰車八輛、陶馬三十二匹。其排列的方法是：戰車與步兵混合編組，排成一個坐西朝東的長方形軍陣。由前鋒、後衛、主體、側翼四部分組成。前鋒，由三排面東的南北向横隊組成，每排六十八件武士俑，三排共二百零四件。前鋒之後，接着是戰車與步兵相間排列的長約184米的大型縱陣，這是軍陣的主體。在其南北兩側各有一排分別爲面南、面北的長約184米的東西向横隊，這是軍陣兩側的翼衛。在俑坑的西端亦有三排南北向的横隊，其中兩排面東，最後一排面西，這是軍陣的後衛，用以防止敵人從後面襲擊。可見此軍陣組織的嚴密。

古代布陣的一個重要原則，就是每個陣都要有鋭利的前鋒隊伍和強大的後續隊伍。如果一個軍隊没有強大的前鋒，就好像一把劍没有劍鋒一樣；如果只有前鋒而没有強大的後續力量，就像劍無柄。只有"有鋒有後"，才能"相信不動，敵人必走"(《孫臏兵法·勢備》)。秦俑軍陣的編列是符合這一原則的。一號俑坑前鋒的武士俑是輕裝打扮，不穿鎧甲，免盔束髮。腿紮行縢，手持弓弩，是能"逾高絶遠，輕足善走"的勇士。一號俑坑在前鋒之後，是戰車和步兵相間排列的三十八路縱陣。這些武士俑都身穿鎧甲，脛縛護腿，手持矛、戈或弓弩等兵器，是屬於重裝的甲士，利於與敵人持久酣戰，格殺斯鬥。一號俑坑軍陣的編列是以輕捷的鋭士在前，重裝的勇士居

後，其前進的衝擊力和持久的拼搏力結合，就形成了巨大的戰鬥力量，能陷堅破鋭、殲頑敵。

一號俑坑東端戰車與步兵的排列方法是：戰車兩兩成雙，即所謂"雙車編組"。雙車中一輛爲主車，另一輛爲副車。防禦時兩車互相掩護，不致左右受敵；進攻時便於對敵形成夾擊。所以兩車不能分離。如果分離了，就變成了"偏師"，一定要打敗仗的。

關於戰車和步兵的結合問題。每輛車上有甲士三人，即一名御手，兩名戰士。車的前後左右都配有步兵。每輛車前的步兵共有三排，每排四人，三排共十二人，組成一個小的戰鬥單位，作爲車的前拒隊。車的左右兩側的步兵人數不等，約爲52－60人。每四人一排，共若干排組成一個長方形的縱隊。行軍時夾轅而行，作戰時在車的兩側各自負責一個側面，成爲車的左右拒隊。車後跟隨的步兵不等，有的爲七十二人，有的百餘人。這種以戰車爲中心在其前後、左右配置步兵的編組方法，即古代的所謂"五陳"隊形。步兵與戰車協同密切，增強了步兵對戰車的掩護能力。這種組合方法體現了以步兵爲主，它適用於防守或在地勢崎嶇戰車不便發揮威力的情況。而在地勢平坦的地區，其陣形又有變化，多以戰車在前、步兵在後。以戰車爲主，步兵起配合輔助作用。即所謂"先偏後伍，伍承彌縫"，"先其車足以當敵，後其人足以待變"(《山堂考索·車戰》)。所以，戰車和步兵的編組方法要視地形及敵人的情況而變化。

2、二號兵馬俑坑軍陣

二號俑坑是個曲形陣，由四個小陣有機結合而組成。

第一個小方陣是個弩兵陣，位於曲形陣的前端，構成軍陣的前角。這個小陣分爲陣表和陣心兩部分。陣表(即方陣的四旁)由一百七十四件立式的弩兵俑組成。這些武士俑都不穿鎧甲，爲輕裝打扮。陣心部分由一百六十件蹲跪式弩兵組成。分作八路縱隊，每路二十件。他們都身穿鎧甲，手控弓弩，爲重裝備。這個小陣爲什麽位於陣表的俑爲立姿，陣心的俑爲跪姿？因爲古代弓弩射擊時，一是要求前無立兵，以免誤傷己方人員；二是要求輪番射擊，以形成矢如雨注的形勢，使敵人無可乘之機。這一小陣的立兵和跪兵，應當是一立一跪、迭次交換、輪番射擊。即陣表的立式兵先射擊，射後即蹲下；然後陣心的兵起立射擊。二者輪番交換，射擊不絶，敵人無法接近。

第二小方陣爲車陣，位於曲形陣的右側。共有八列戰車組成，每列八輛，共六十四輛戰車。每輛戰車前駕有四馬，車上有甲士三人，其中一人爲御手，另二人爲戰士。車的前後左右没有配置步兵。這與殷周乃至春秋時代的戰車都不相同。那時的每輛戰車一定要有步兵跟隨。這種編列方法，是過去我們所不知道的一個變化。其變化的原因，是因爲戰國和秦王朝時步兵已成爲獨立的兵種，作戰時是車、步、騎混合編組，所以每輛戰車就不必一定要有隸屬步兵了。

第三個小陣是戰車和步兵騎兵相結合排列的縱陣，位於曲形陣的中部。計有戰車十九輛，分成三路縱隊。第一路和第三路各有戰車六輛，二路有戰車七輛。每輛車上有甲士三人，其中一名爲御手，兩名戰士。第三路縱隊最後的一輛戰車，是本車隊的指揮車，上有將軍俑一件。車後配置有步兵。前邊的戰車每輛車後配置步兵八人，後邊的戰車後配步兵二十八人或三十二人。末尾的殿軍是兩組騎兵和三十二名步兵。騎兵每組四騎，共八騎。三十二名步兵分作八排，每排四人，組成一個縱長方形的梯隊位於最末一輛戰車之後。在車陣中出現騎兵，也是我們過去所不知道的軍陣編列中的一個變化。騎兵行動輕捷，可以作爲軍陣中的機動兵用，這就增強了車陣的靈活性。

第四個小陣是騎兵陣，位於曲形陣的左側。由六輛戰車和一百零八個騎兵組成一個長方形的縱陣。這個縱陣分爲陣頭和陣體兩部分。陣頭是兩列戰車中間夾一列騎兵。戰車每列三輛，車上有乘員二人，其中一名御手、一名車右。騎兵一列分爲三組，每組四騎，計十二騎。陣體是由八列騎兵組成，每列亦爲三組，一組四騎，八列共

九十六騎。總計此騎兵陣共有馬一百零八匹，每匹馬前立有牽馬的騎士俑一件。

上面分述的四個小陣有機地合成一個大陣。這種佈陣方法，兵書上叫作大陣套小陣，大營包小營，陣中有陣，營中有營，偶落鈎連，折曲相對。一個大陣中如果不包小陣，則機動靈活性差，造成"兵不可復分"，一旦碰到複雜的地形和不同的敵情，則兵卒擁擠，兵力難以展開和難於轉換隊形。

四個小陣擺列的位置，是弩兵居前，三個側面接敵，便於發揮強弩的威力。車陣居右，正面和右側兩面接敵，正面又有弩兵的交叉掩護，攻、守都很方便。騎兵居左，僅左側一面接敵，防守時三面得到掩護，進攻時便於離合。車、步、騎結合的另一小陣居中，其後尾成爲殿軍。這實際上還是前、後、左、右、中五陣鈎連，互相掩應。分開各自成爲一個戰鬥分隊，合起來成爲一個多兵種的軍陣。分合的變化，在於指揮官靈活運用，變化無窮。

車、步、騎三個兵種混合編組，這是戰國以來軍陣的一個重要變化。在此以前的軍陣僅為車陣，自步兵、騎兵成爲獨立的兵種後才出現了這種變化。車、步、騎三者的作用不同，戰車用以"險堅陣，要強敵，遮走北"；騎兵作為機動兵，用以蹂敗軍、絕糧道、擊便寇；在車騎不易施展威力的險峻窄狹或沼澤區，和扼守要塞時則多用步兵。《孫臏兵法·八陣》說："車騎與戰者，分以為三，一在於右，一在於左，一在於後。易則多其車，險則多其騎，厄則多其弩。險易必知生地、死地，居生擊死"。這段話的意思是說，車、步、騎三者混合編隊，根據地形和敵情來確定作戰時以哪一種兵種為主，哪一種兵種為輔。三者緊密配合才能打勝仗。如公元前262年秦國和楚國的長平之戰，秦國的三個兵種配合得宜，先把一支步兵埋伏下來，正面的部隊佯裝敗退。趙軍貿然追擊，伏兵斷其後路，又出騎兵五千，突然插入趙軍的營壘間，把趙軍分割包圍，終於殲滅趙軍四十五萬人。這是車、步、騎混合作戰最典型的戰例之一。

3. 三號兵馬俑坑衛兵的編列

三號俑坑是一個指揮部，出土戰車一輛，武士俑六十八件。車前駕四馬，車後立武士俑四件，其中一名為御手，二名甲士，一名軍吏。北側的廂房內有武士俑二十二件，分作兩邊相向而立夾道排列，每邊十一件。南側的走廊、過道、前廳、後室內，分別有武士俑八件、六件、二十四件、四件，都分作兩半相向而立夾道排列。這種排列方法顯然不是戰鬥隊形的編組，而是衛隊的排列。他們手中拿的兵器是殳。殳是一種護身的儀衛兵器。這說明三號兵馬俑坑內的武士俑都是衛士，這是一個警衛隊。

一、二、三號兵馬俑坑都不是孤立的，而是互相聯繫的、有機地組合在一起的一個軍陣編列的整體。一號俑坑是右軍，二號俑坑為左軍，另外還有個上面提到的未建成的俑坑是原計劃中的中軍，三號坑為統帥左、右、中三軍的指揮部。這個軍陣編列的整體，可以認爲是秦國軍隊編組的縮影，是古代軍陣的一種圖解，是一部活的兵書，在軍事史上具有極重要的科學價值。

五 秦俑藝術

秦俑不但以數量多、形體大惹人矚目，更以它那生動的形象，渾厚雄大和明快洗練的藝術風格、藝術技巧，耐人尋味，使人百看不厭。秦俑是已經成熟了的中國古典藝術作品，和秦以前的雕塑藝術比較，它繼承了過去一些優良的傳統並發揚光大，把雕塑藝術水平提高到新的高度，進入到一個新的發展時期。秦俑藝術對後代來說，是個榜樣。它承前啟後，在中國雕塑史上具有劃時代的意義。

(一) 秦俑藝術的寫實風格

秦俑之所以能引起人們的矚目，得到人們的喜歡，具有"永久的魅力"，是因爲它真實地反映了社會生活，塑造了成千上萬個秦軍將士的逼真形象。每一個秦俑都似一個有血有肉、有情感和性格

的人物，而不是矯揉造作虛構的一群無生命的偶像。

秦俑的個性鮮明，數千武士俑的面貌各不相同。有的是長方面龐，寬寬的額頭，高高的顴骨，粗眉大眼，鬢髯開張，性格剛毅勇猛。有的面龐圓潤豐滿，五官端莊，胸懷豁達，性格爽朗。有的是橢圓形的面龐，五官清秀，性格文雅。有的方方的面龐，容顏渾厚，性格憨直質樸。有的眉如山脊，目光炯炯，銳氣逼人，似有超人的大勇。有的劍眉圓眼，鬍角翻卷，顯得怒氣衝衝。有的眉清目秀，兩片板狀小鬍翹翹撅起，顯得機敏伶俐。人的年齡不同，面容和神情也就不一樣。一般額頭有皺紋的年齡大的武士俑，面容端莊，神情嚴肅，好像是飽經風霜、富有生活閱歷的老戰士；年輕的小戰士，一般都是胖鼓鼓的臉蛋，笑咪咪的，帶着天真的稚氣。

秦俑藝術比較成功的地方，還在它塑造了各種不同身份的人物典型。其中有高級、中級和低級軍吏，以及各種不同職掌的戰士。

將軍俑，個個身材高大魁梧，身穿雙重長襦，外披彩色魚鱗甲，足登翹尖履，頭戴鶡冠，衣飾華麗，氣宇不凡。有的面目清秀，一把長鬚，神態雍容。他右手拇指與食指相捏，通過這個細小動作描寫了他的足智多謀，胸懷雄兵百萬的氣度。有的是長方形的面龐，絡腮大鬍，神態威武。他雙手拄劍，昂首挺立，威風凜凜。人們可以想象到他那揮軍前進，馳騁沙場的英姿。有的面龐寬綽，容顏渾厚，胸懷廣闊。那額頭上起伏的皺紋，顯現了他身經百戰的廣博閱歷。將軍的職責在於指揮，而不在一劍之勇。秦朝的法律規定，統軍的將領不得衝到陣前斬敵人的首級，否則要受流放的懲罰。所以秦俑坑出土的將軍俑只有衛體的武器——劍，而沒有持其它兵器者。在氣度上，都顯現出是多謀善斷，剛毅果敢的將領，具有知天、知地、知此知彼，胸操勝算的將才。

中級軍吏俑，都身穿長襦，外披帶彩色花邊的護胸甲或齊邊甲，頭戴長冠。人們不但可以通過那與眾不同的服飾知道其地位的高低，而且在姿態和氣度上亦可一望而知。有的站在將軍俑的一旁，面容嚴肅，神態恭謹，好像是將軍的副手。有的身材高大，神情肅穆，那三滴水式的髭鬚和凝聚的眉宇，顯得意志堅定而有自信力。他左手握劍，右手似在執桴靜候軍令。只要一聲令下，他即可擂鼓揮軍前進。金鼓為軍隊的耳目，"鼓之則進，重鼓則擊"，鼓音不絕，則大軍冒矢雨，犯白刃，滾滾向前。銳不可當。

下級軍吏俑的數量很多，不便一一論述，這裏只舉出幾個典型。例如一號兵馬俑坑東端的前鋒部隊，共有二百多件武士俑，其中有兩件與眾不同。一件位於前鋒部隊的左側(隊末)，他身高1.97米，膀寬腰圓，身穿鎧甲，頭戴長冠，左手似按着寶劍，右手作持戈、矛等長兵器的姿勢，威風凜凜地挺立着。那緊抿的嘴唇，凝聚的眼神，顯得意志剛強如鐵。那嚴肅的面容、恭謹的神態，恰與它的身份相稱，他是個嚴於職守的下級軍吏。在前鋒部隊的右側，即隊首有一件軍吏俑。他頭戴長冠，身上沒有穿鎧甲，是輕裝打扮。他左手握劍，右手執長兵，鼓腹昂首，性格慓悍。一旦和敵人拼搏起來，一定是個身先士卒的好漢。

各兵種的武士俑，因職掌不同而姿態各殊。如二號兵馬俑坑第一試掘方出土的戰車上的三件武士俑，在車後作一字形排列，中間為御手，兩側分別為車左和車右。御手身微前傾，雙臂向前平舉，雙手半握拳作用力攬轡狀。他面容嚴肅，神情集中，眼睛緊緊盯住車前輅駕的四匹駿馬。　左邊的一件武士俑，右足向前跨半步作稍息姿勢；左手持長兵，右臂衣袖縮至肘部，右手作用力按車狀；頭微微向右側轉，傾耳凝神，似在聽令。右邊的一件武士俑，姿態與之相反，左足向前出半步作稍息姿勢，右手執長兵，左臂衣袖縮至肘部，左手作用力按車狀，頭微向左側轉，昂首傾耳凝神。車前輅駕的四馬，舉頸仰首，張口嘶鳴，攢蹄欲行。馬的躍躍欲動，御手緊握馬轡的欲靜，兩名戰士的凝神聽令，和諧地組成了一幅整裝待發的生動畫面。似乎只要一聲令下，戰士即騰躍登車，御手揚鞭，四馬奮蹄，馳驅疆場。秦代的雕塑大師把人與人、人與馬之間的姿態、神情，巧妙地

融爲一體，互相輝映，静中寓動。把人們的視綫從有限的空間引到無限的疆場，意境深遠。

二號俑坑東端弩兵組成的方陣，有立姿和跪姿兩種武士俑。立姿的一百七十四件武士俑，都作輕裝打扮，立於方陣四週。這些武士俑的姿態非常寫實和生動。它們的左足都向左前方跨半步，雙足略呈丁字形站立。左腿前弓，右腿後绷；身體微向左側轉，左臂平舉伸掌，右臂曲舉於胸前；眼睛盯視左前方，绷着嘴，鼓着勁，似在用力練習持弩的動作。《吳越春秋》記載，越王對陳音説："願復聞正射之道"。陳音對曰："臣聞射之道，左足縱，右足橫，左手若拊枝，右手若抱兒，右手發，右手不知，此正射持弩之道也。"所謂"右手發，右手不知"，即眼睛的注意力始終集中在箭鏃瞄準的目的物上，不要回視扣扳機的右手。文獻和實物對照基本吻合。秦俑的姿態動作完全是按照弩兵射擊要領的動作塑造的。擺在人們面前的好像一羣真實的弩兵，在認真地一絲不苟地進行習練。觀覽這些秦俑，我們既得到了美的享受，又學到了古代兵法的知識。位於方陣中部的一百六十件武士俑，爲穿鎧甲的重裝兵。都作蹲跪的姿勢，即左腿蹲曲，右膝跪地，右臂前曲，左臂曲舉於胸前，雙手一上一下作用力控弓的姿態。身體微向左邊側轉，仰首警惕地注視左前方。方陣的左右角並排站立着一件將軍俑和一件中級軍吏俑。它們那雙足八字立，舉目掃視前方。那嚴肅的面龐，鋭利的目光，好像一條無形的綫，把整個方陣三百餘件武士俑的動作、神情串連起來。人們通過這條無形的綫，彷彿看到秦軍戰士隨着將帥的號令，在進行着"圓而方之，坐而起之，行而止之，左而右之，前而後之，分而合之，結而解之"的陣形變化的隊列操練，以及單兵持弩發弩動作的基本訓練。這是一幅生動的"教戰圖"。看到這些武士俑練兵的情況，使人們不由得想起中國古代的軍事家孫子練兵的故事。一天，吳王闔閭要親眼看看孫子如何練兵，選宫中美女一百八十八人，叫孫子小試練兵。孫子把宫女分爲二隊，以王的寵妾二人各爲隊長，皆令持戟，令之曰："你們知道心與左右手背嗎？"婦人答道："知道。"孫子又説："前則視心，左視左手，右視右手，後即視背。"婦人答道："是。"三令五申以後，孫子於是"鼓之右"，婦人大笑。孫子説："約束不明，申令不熟，將之罪。"復三令五申，"而鼓之左"，婦人又大笑。孫子説："約束不明，申令不熟，將之罪也。既已明而不如法者，吏士之罪也。"乃欲斬左右隊長。吳王從臺上看到要斬其愛姬，大駭，趕忙下令説："寡人非此二姬食不甘味，願勿斬也。"孫子説："臣既已受命爲將，將在軍，君命有所不受"，遂斬隊長二人以殉，用其次爲隊長。於是復鼓之。婦人左右前後跪起，皆中規矩繩墨，無敢出聲。於是孫子使報王曰："兵既整齊，王可試下觀之。唯王所欲用之，雖赴水火猶可也。"古代軍事家非常重視練兵。所謂"士不選練，卒不服習，起居不精，動静不集，趨利弗及，避難不畢，前擊後解，與金鼓之指相失，此不習勒卒之過也，百不當十"(《漢書·爰盎鼂錯列傳》卷49)。秦將王翦率六十萬大軍攻楚時，先讓士卒修整操練，而後終於獲得大勝。秦弩兵俑的習戰羣塑，反映了秦的嚴於治軍思想。三百餘件武士俑動作合乎規矩繩墨，個個神情嚴肅認真，生氣勃勃，好像皆是"雖赴水火猶可"的訓練有素的戰士。

綜上所言，秦俑的姿態多種多樣，各兵種的人物典型都性格鮮明。但是在個性鮮明的數千武士俑的形象中，又有着相同的共性——"勇於公戰，怯於私鬥"。這是一支富有朝氣的英勇頑强的精鋭軍隊。這是剛剛登上歷史舞臺不久的新興地主階級的精神面貌，在雕塑藝術上的體現。透過秦俑羣雕，我們可以看到那個時代的精神面貌，它的意境是宏闊的，風格是寫實的，不愧爲中國最優秀的現實主義的古典雕塑藝術作品。

(二) 秦俑的藝術風格和藝術技巧

秦俑藝術不同於西方的雕塑藝術，它的表現手法比較含蓄，感情是内向的，着重通過面部的五官來揭示人物的内心世界，風格質樸雄厚，内在的力量好像大海的波濤，一浪接一浪洶湧澎湃，蘊藏着雄偉博大的凝聚力量。

秦俑藝術，具體説有以下幾點鮮明的特徵：

首先，在題材的處理和總體佈局方面，它是以塑造左、中、右三軍軍陣的編列作爲宏偉的構圖。以軍隊爲題材的雕塑過去也發現了不少，但以秦俑這樣形體之大、數量之多的雕塑，在中國和世界雕塑史上是没有任何作品可以與之相比的。千軍萬馬，氣勢磅礴，其藝術的感染力較一般的小構圖要深遠、宏大得多。在題材的處理方面，它不是選取兩軍的白刃格鬥，也不是漢唐石刻和壁畫中常見的車馬儀仗的隊列，而是捕捉了三軍的整裝待發、躍躍欲戰的一瞬間。這樣處理比較含蓄，意境遼闊。秦軍在疆場上叱咤風雲的驚心動魄的戰鬥情景，雖没有直接描繪，但却意在其中了。所以它給人們的不單是視覺的觀賞，而且引起人們思想的馳騁，耐人反復地玩味。

再者，在藝術技巧方面，它不求細微末節的真實，而是抓住關鍵的部位運用藝術的誇張和提煉概括的技法着意塑造。例如，陶俑軀幹部分的塑造比較概括，僅求其形似，衣紋簡潔，無繁縟的虚飾。但那雙肩寬綽，腹圓如鼓，衣褶飛散，顯然是經過了誇張。這既表現了秦國戰士體魄健壯、力可扛鼎的勇士形象，又使軀幹有一定的旋律。由於衣褶呈盤口形，在造型上增强了立如鐵塔的穩固感和力量感。有的衣褶向後飛撒，如在强風中挺立，更烘托了戰士大無畏的精神氣質。陶俑頭部的雕塑手法細膩，五官的刻畫尤爲精緻傳神。如通過那凝聚的眼眉，緊閉的嘴唇，表現了人物的意志剛毅堅定。炯炯的目光，眉間的肌肉攥成疙瘩，表現了人物性格的粗獷和勇猛的氣質。眉宇舒緩，目光下視，表現了人物性格的文静靦覥。雙唇半啟，嘴角上挑，眼睛半眯，刻畫了人物的和顏悦色。上身微向前傾，張口瞠目，顯現了神情的驚愕。眉毛和鬍鬚都經過藝術的誇張，使人物的形象更明快清晰。如眉毛塑得粗大，鬍鬚塑得飛起來、立起來、翻卷起來。如果從解剖學的角度看，是不符合實際的。但是藝術效果使人們並不感到不真實，反而更感到人物性格的鮮明和突出。當人們看到那滿臉絡腮大鬍的陶俑，立即感到這個人物性格豪放。看到那像牛犄角似的雙角翹翹的大鬍，就感到這個人物性格慓悍。看到那三滴水式的乳狀髭鬚，就感到這個人物的性格與衆不同，有點桀驁不馴。看到那兩片小小的平八字鬍，就感到這個人物性格的機敏。那長鬚飄撒在胸前，烘托了人物風度的瀟灑。秦俑鬍鬚的類型，粗略地統計一下，約有二十餘種，每一種都和五官的神情相互呼應。眼睛是心靈的一扇窗子，透過這扇窗子可以窺見人物的内心世界，這是秦俑着意刻畫的重點。但藉助鬍鬚來烘托人物的性格，和眼神的刻畫相配合來表現人物的氣質和精神面貌，也是秦俑藝術的獨到之處。

秦俑藝術的雕塑手法是寫實的。武士俑的形象是以秦王朝真實的士兵爲模特兒塑造的，服裝、甲衣都逼真，其基本結構與實物無異。通過士兵的容貌甚至可以看出士兵來源哪些地區。如那闊額、厚唇、寬腮，性格愨厚純樸的形象，一定是個來自關中地區的秦卒。那圓臉、尖下巴，神情機敏的形象，好像是個巴蜀人。那高顴骨、寬耳輪、薄眼皮、結實、强悍的形象，又像是個隴東人。秦軍的成分主要是關中的秦人，亦雜有其它地區的少數民族，這點是與歷史事實相符的。秦俑的寫實不是照相的翻版，而是經過藝術的加工，使其形象更加典型化。

秦俑藝術，裝飾性的手法也有不少體現。那用梳狀工具刮劃出來的髮絲，用棒狀工具刮劃的螺旋形髮紋，都具有較濃的裝飾意味。裝飾性是中國古代青銅器造型上常用的手法，秦俑藝術繼承了這一藝術傳統，並把圓雕、浮雕、綫雕有機地結合，運用塑、堆、捏、貼、刻、畫等民間畫工常用的"六法"，來顯示立體形象的體、量、形、神、色、質等藝術效果。秦俑藝術可以説是集中了我國民族雕塑藝術傳統技法的大成，對後世的雕塑藝術有着巨大的影響。

從解剖學的角度觀察，秦俑雖然還有一些幼稚的地方，有的比例失調，製作粗糙，但絕大多數秦俑各部位的比例還是適宜的，骨節、肌肉的關係，處理得比較合理。

總的說來，秦俑藝術是成熟的優秀作品，反映了出身於社會下層的藝術匠師深邃的觀察力和卓越的表現能力，是我國古代雕塑史上的一顆明珠。標誌着我國的雕塑藝術至秦代已進入一個嶄新的發展時期，對漢唐以至後代的雕塑藝術的發展產生了深遠的影響，在雕塑史上具有劃時代的意義。

(三)陶俑、陶馬的製作工藝

陶俑、陶馬的製作工藝，從大的方面說來可以分爲雕塑、焙燒、繪彩三大工序。而每一道工序中又有許多製作的工藝過程。爲了把問題說得比較清楚、明確，分別予以叙述。

1. 雕塑

雕塑陶俑、陶馬的用料需經過精心地選擇和調治。土，選用的是驪山北麓的黃土和白色的石英砂。把土經過篩選和淘洗，清除雜質，以便使燒出的陶俑、陶馬質地純净、色澤均匀。把石英砂碾成細小的顆粒，按照適當的比例和土摻合，加水調匀。再經過反復地揉練、捶打，使泥軟硬適宜。

陶俑的製作，首先塑成粗胎，然後再進行精心的細部刻畫。粗胎是由下而上逐漸叠型。具體說來：第一步先用模具做出長、寬各約32厘米，厚約3－4厘米的方形足踏板。有的在做足踏板的同時即塑造雙足；有的是足踏板與俑的雙足分做，然後粘合在一起。第二步，在雙足的後跟接上雙腿。腿有實心腿和空心腿兩種。實心腿是用泥卷搓成型，空心腿是用卷泥片法製作。第三步，在雙腿的上部包裹泥片做成的短褲，待稍微陰乾後，再在上部覆泥塑成軀幹下部的底盤。第四步，在軀幹底盤上用泥條盤築法塑造軀幹。軀幹一般是分作兩段製作，即第一次先塑造腰部以下的部分，待稍微陰乾後再接着塑造軀幹的上部。也有的是從腰部分爲上下兩段，分別做好後再互相套接粘合成一體。第五步，制作陶俑的雙臂，有的是單獨制作再粘接於胸腔兩側相應的位置；有的是在胸腔的兩側接塑雙臂。第六步，頭和手預先分別單做，再與軀幹套合粘接。頭部粗胎的做法比較複雜，方法不一，簡單說，是先用模具造頭的大型，再在頭頂、腦後堆泥塑造髮辮、髮髻，再粘接上雙耳、脖頸，仔細地刻畫五官、鬍鬚、髮絲。塑造頭的初胎所用的模具，有單模和雙模兩種，其中以用雙模做者最多。雙模是把頭分爲大小相等的前後兩片半模。兩片半模分別填泥做好後，再把兩片半模鬥合粘接在一起，形成頭部的大樣。單模，形狀呈橢圓餅形，是用以製作顏面部分的。其餘部分是用手捏塑成瓢形的腦殼，把單模製作的顏面部分粘接到捏塑的瓢形腦殼上面，再接上脖頸，粘接上耳朵，即形成了頭的大樣。耳朵係用單模製作。頭上的圓形髮髻，有的是用手捏塑，有的是用雙模製作後粘接於頭頂。

手部粗胎的做法也是多種多樣，伸掌者多數採用雙模製作；半握拳者有的是捏塑成型，有的是模、塑結合。即手掌部分用模，手指部分爲捏塑。

通過上述六個步驟，陶俑的粗胎基本上形成。然後就要進行細部的雕飾刻畫。在雕飾刻畫以前，先要在粗胎上塗一層薄薄的細泥，也有的不再進行二次覆泥，而把粗胎的表面經過刮削、打光磨平。軀幹部分的雕刻手法洗練概括，風格粗獷，綫條簡潔。衣服的褶紋、領口和袖頭的鑲緣，都用陰綫刻表示。大的褶紋用粗綫，複雜的褶紋用細綫，繁簡、粗細適宜，層次豐富。鎧甲多數是減地法作成淺浮雕的效果，也有的是覆泥雕刻而成。甲衣上的甲釘和連甲帶是用單模押印做成。甲衣的雕刻都用筆直的綫條，以表現甲片的硬直，衣紋多用流動的曲綫以表現衣服質地的輕軟。

頭、手、足、腿等部分的雕飾手法比較細膩。頭部的髮辮採用減地法或貼泥片法做出淺浮雕的效果，上面再用陰綫刻。髮髻採用圓雕、浮雕和綫刻的技法，形象逼真。髮絲的雕飾手法多樣，有的是用梳狀的工具刮劃出縷縷的髮絲。有的是用棒狀的工具刮劃成一圈

圈的規整的螺旋紋，類似隋唐時期佛像的螺髻。有的是先做成高低波浪起伏的浮雕效果，上面再加陰綫刻。前兩種髮紋裝飾意味較濃，後一種手法做的髮紋質感較强。面部的五官是着意雕刻的重點。眉骨，有的刻成高浮雕，形如山岳，藉以表現人物的勇敢强悍。有的眉骨爲淺浮雕，上面加陰綫刻出眉絲。眼睛，上眼皮壓下眼皮，內眼角低外眼角高，都交待得清晰。憤怒者，雙目圓睜；微笑者，眼睛半眯。眼睛是心靈的窗子，刻畫得比較精細傳神。年老者面上有皺起的褶紋，年輕者面龐圓潤豐滿。面部肌肉與神情關係的處理和諧、合理。鬍鬚的種類很多，雕造的手法有的用堆法，有的用貼法，有的爲減地刻法等，先做成鬍鬚的大型，再用細綫刻出鬚絲。總之，面龐細部的刻畫，風格細膩，神態生動，表現了人物的不同性格和精神面貌。

手的細部刻畫，符合解剖原理。手指節的長短粗細、肌肉的厚薄、筋骨的伸曲等，都處理得合情合理。脚和腿經過刮削打磨和精心地刻畫，顯示了筋骨的硬直和肌肉的厚薄。脚掌內側高外側低，直立者腿圓，綳腿者腿扁，這些細節表現得惟妙惟肖。

陶馬的製作也是先做成粗胎，然後再進行細部的雕飾。陶馬粗胎的做法是：

第一步，預製陶馬的頭、頸、軀幹、腿、耳、尾等部件。頭是藉助模具成型，即從頭的中間分成左右兩片半模，兩片分做後粘合在一起。嘴的下巴是單獨用手捏塑插接上去的。腿部的陶質密度大、堅硬如石，説明在製作的過程中經過反復地捶打加壓。頸和軀幹部分是預先製作成若干塊泥片，以便拼裝組合時應用。頸部一般是由左右兩片泥合成；軀幹分爲臀、腹、胸三段，每段由三片或四片泥片鬥合而成。馬的耳朵、尾巴都是捏塑成型。

第二步，把預先製作的陶馬的各個部件進行拼裝組合。首先把預製的四條腿立在固定的位置上，並搭好承托軀幹部分泥片的支撐架，以承托軀幹部分的壓力，減輕四條腿的負重量，以免四肢受壓變形或移位。接着在四肢和支撐架上鋪設預先製作的軀幹部分的泥片。先放下部的泥片，再疊兩側的泥片，最後覆蓋上部的泥片。猶如蓋房一樣，先打地基，再砌邊牆，最後蓋頂。泥片與泥片之間用泥粘接，並在內側合縫縫上敷泥加固，經過捶打使合縫密實成爲一個整體。爲了防止腹腔變形，內部要用支撐板撐持。待軀幹的大型做好後，再依次接上脖頸、頭，在臀部插上尾巴。在每一個合縫縫上都要敷泥加固和反復捶打，使合縫堅實。在接脖頸和頭部時要用丁字形支架承托，以防下墜。

經過上述工序，馬體的粗胎(或叫大樣)基本成型。在粗胎上塗一層細泥後開始進行細部的雕飾。馬的四肢經過刮削和刻畫，以表現四肢勁健；臀部經過磨光打平，來顯示馬的腰肥、臀部滾瓜溜圓。在胸部堆貼泥塊以雕造隆突的胸肌。馬的頭部，用曲017陰綫刻畫眼皮、鼻翼、口角等處的褶紋。眼球的週圍刻鏤較深，使眼球暴起好像銅鈴一樣，炯炯有神。從整體看來，馬的造型準確，各部分的比例適宜，軀幹部分沒有過多的雕飾，表現手法簡潔。四肢如刀削斧砍，硬面和直綫條很多，風格粗獷，技法熟練。頭部窄長瘦削，透皮見骨。陶馬的塑造似出於技藝高超匠師之手，是秦俑中的精品。

陶俑、陶馬的塑造，從技法上來看，熟練地運用了塑、堆、捏、貼、刻、畫等民間匠師常用的"六法"，以顯示立體形象的體、量、形、神、色、質等藝術效果。大的立體形象是用塑、堆的技法做成圓雕，表現形象的體、量、形。立體上的裝飾用堆、捏、貼等技法做成浮雕。立體上的細部用刻畫的綫雕技法，以表現形象的神情、氣質。從而使立體形象層次豐富和個性鮮明。遠在兩千多年以前，已能如此熟練地掌握雕塑的各種技法，並形成了我國民族雕塑的一套傳統技巧，充分顯示了秦代勞動人民的聰明才智，表明秦代的雕塑藝術已提高到了一個新的水平。

2. 焙燒和繪彩

陶俑、陶馬雕塑成型，待陰乾後放進窰內焙燒。燒製陶俑和陶

馬的窯址目前還沒有發掘，結構情況還不清楚。秦代燒磚瓦的窯多為半地下式，由窯室、火膛、火門等部分組成。窯室有方形、三角形、馬蹄形等。後兩種窯室較小，方形窯室較大，面積約5平方米。陶俑、陶馬的體形大，可能是利用方形窯燒的。

焙燒的關鍵在於掌握火候的高低。《天工開物》講到燒磚問題時說：“凡火候少一兩，則鏽色不光；少三兩，則名嫩火磚，本色雜現，他日經霜冒雪，則立成解散，仍還土質。火候多一兩，則磚面有裂紋；多三兩，則磚型縮小折裂，屈曲不伸，擊之如碎鐵然，不適於用”。秦俑坑出土的陶俑、陶馬，火候勻，色澤純（呈青灰色），硬度大，沒有沒燒透的夾生現象，也沒有燒過了的折裂、變形現象。說明焙燒的火候恰到好處。經測定，陶俑、陶馬是經過大約九百至一千攝氏度的高溫燒成的。如此高大的陶塑，胚胎由濕變乾及入窯焙燒，都有一定的收縮系數，掌握不好也要變形。焙燒秦俑的匠師原來都是有經驗的陶工，在長期的生產實踐中積累了豐富的經驗，因而能較成功地掌握陶塑的收縮比例，反映了秦代燒窯工藝水平的高超。陶俑、陶馬身體各部的胎壁厚薄不一。如陶俑的腹腔和胸腔部分的胎壁厚約2－3厘米，而衣的下擺及腿部厚達10餘厘米。陶馬的腹腔一般厚約2－4厘米，腿根部則厚約10－15厘米。由於厚薄不均，很容易造成薄的地方燒好了，而厚的地方還沒有燒透；或者厚的地方燒好了，而薄的地方則燒過。爲了解決這個問題，雕塑的匠師想了很多巧妙的方法，如多留過火孔道，在厚的部位鑽孔、挖溝槽，或者做成空心、夾層等等，以盡量減少泥層的厚度，達到各部分火候均勻的目的。

陶俑、陶馬經過焙燒後，通體的顏色呈青灰色。爲了表現不同的服色和衣服上的花紋，在陶胎上再進行繪彩。因俑坑經過火燒和埋在地下兩千多年水土的侵蝕，陶俑和陶馬身上原來的色彩基本已全部剝落，僅存殘迹，只有極個別的顏色保存較好，色澤如新。目前已發現的陶俑、陶馬身上顏色的種類有朱紅、棗紅、粉紅、綠、粉綠、粉紫、藍、粉藍、中黃、橘黃、黑、白、赭等色。顏色的質地都是礦物。施色的方法，是先塗一層明膠作底，以便增强顏色的附着力，然後在底色上敷彩。

二號兵馬俑坑試掘方內出土的幾件陶俑、陶馬身上的顏色保存較好，使我們大體可以看到色彩的原貌。例如：二號俑坑第四試掘方出土的將軍俑，上穿朱紅色中衣，外套深紫色長襦，袖口和領部鑲着朱紅色花邊。上身穿着彩色魚鱗甲，赭色甲片，配着朱紅色甲釘和連甲帶。甲衣的週邊、領口和前後胸部，滿綴着精緻的彩色圖案花紋。甲衣的雙肩部分，週圍嵌着花邊，中部以米黃色作底，上繪兩個藍色花朵。甲衣的前後胸各有三個用彩帶紮的花結，雙肩各有一朵，帶尾飄撒。將軍俑的下身穿粉綠色長褲，脚穿赭色翹尖鞋，頭戴深紫色鶡冠，冠上繫着橘黃色冠帶。它雙手交垂於腹前作拄劍貌，昂首挺胸，氣宇軒昂。

和上一件將軍俑同時出土的還有一件地位較將軍俑略低的中級軍吏俑。它身穿綠色長襦，緄鑲着朱紅色的領緣和袖緣。外披的護胸甲，赭色甲片，配着朱紅色的甲釘和甲帶。甲衣的週邊鑲着白色邊緣。領緣和背帶上繪着幾何形的彩色圖案花紋。下身穿棗紅色長襦，足穿赭黑色翹尖鞋，頭戴赭色長冠。臉、手、足塗粉紅色。眉毛、鬍鬚用墨綫描畫。眼睛繪着白睛黑珠，炯炯有神。

二號兵馬俑坑第十試掘方出土的一件蹲跪式的武士俑，身穿綠色長襦，押着朱紅色的領緣和袖緣，外披赭色鎧甲，綴着朱紅色甲釘和甲帶。下着深藍色長褲，紮着粉紫色護腿，赭色鞋上鑲着粉紫色口緣，頭上綰着圓髻，髻上紮着朱紅色髮帶。

陶馬身上的顏色比較簡單，都是平塗的棗紅色，只有鬃和尾巴塗黑色，蹄甲爲白色。

秦俑彩繪的色調總的來看是明快、絢麗。上衣有朱紅、棗紅、綠、粉綠、深紫、粉紫、粉藍等等。一般是紅色的上衣配着綠色或藍色的下衣；綠色或藍色的上衣則配着紅色的下衣。顏色的氣氛熱烈，

進一步烘托了雄偉、壯觀的軍陣陣容。秦俑以繪塑結合，取得了二者相得益彰的藝術效果。

六　秦俑的作者

秦始皇陵兵馬俑的作者是誰？八千兵馬俑是多少人製作的？這是人們比較關心和不易索解的問題。筆者根據多年來在發掘、修復過程中的觀察，發現在一些陶俑、陶馬身上的隱蔽處留有作者的名字——或刻劃或戳印而成。這些陶俑的製作者原來都是處於秦王朝社會下層的陶工。這些陶工有的來源於中央宮廷的製陶作坊，有的來源於地方民間的製陶作坊。截至目前已發現陶工名字八十個，他們都是具有豐富實踐經驗、技藝卓越的陶工工師。每個工師的下面都有一批助手和徒工。以每個工師下面有助手和徒工十餘人計，則八千兵馬俑的製作者約近千人。是一支龐大的雕塑藝術大軍。這些埋沒了兩千多年的藝術大師，今天重現於世，在中國和世界文化藝術史上無疑具有重要的意義。

（一）塑造秦俑的陶工

一、二、三號兵馬俑坑已出土的陶俑、陶馬身上刻劃或戳印的文字，除編號外，大都是陶工的工師名。這些人名大體可分作四類：一是在人名前都冠一“宮”字，簡稱爲“宮”字類；二是在人名前冠一“右”字或“大”字，省稱爲“右”字和“大”字類；三是在人名前冠一地方名；四是僅有人名。第一、二類是來源於中央官府製陶作坊的陶工工師；第三類是來源於地方製陶手工業作坊的陶工工師；第四類因僅有人名，其來源尚難作出確切的判斷。

1、“宮”字類陶工

“宮”字類陶工名，大多數爲戳印的文字，少數爲刻文。目前計發現人名十個，即宮疆、宮得、宮係、宮臧、宮欶、宮頗、宮朝、宮魏、宮犢、宮肤 等。這些人名前都有一個宮字。秦中央有一專門爲宮廷服務的官署機構，名叫“宮水”。其主要職責是爲宮殿建築和陵園建築燒造磚瓦。在秦始皇陵園出土的磚瓦上，亦發現許多“宮”字類的陶工名。如宮疆、宮得、宮係、宮臧、宮欶、宮肤等人名。這些人名既見於兵馬俑坑出土的陶俑身上，又見於始皇陵出土的磚瓦上，絕非偶然的巧合。兵馬俑坑是始皇陵園建築的一部分。兵馬俑的製作時間和陵園建築所用磚瓦的燒造時間相隔不會太遠。因而兵馬俑身上和磚瓦上相同的陶工名，應是同一人。說明這些製作兵馬俑的陶工，本來是燒造磚瓦的工匠。他們是中央宮廷內一批富有經驗的優秀陶工，被抽調出來從事兵馬俑的製作。

2、“大”字和“右”字類陶工

“大”字類的陶文目前計發現三件，即大匧、匠、大邋。前二件見於一號兵馬俑坑出土的陶俑上，後一件見於二號兵馬俑坑的陶俑上。這三種陶文亦見於秦始皇陵園出土的磚瓦上；另外磚瓦上還發現“大匠”二字。大匠是將作大匠的省文。《漢書·百官公卿表》記載：“將作少府，秦官，掌治宮室……景帝中六年（公元前144年）更名將作大匠”。從陶文可知“將作大匠”這一中央官署機構秦代似已存在，其主要職責是負責建造宮室，掌管土木工程及燒造磚瓦。秦始皇陵兵馬俑坑出土的陶俑上的大匧、大邋、匠等陶文中的“大”和“匠”，都是將作大匠的簡稱，而“匧”和“邋”是“將作大匠”統轄下的製陶作坊內的工匠名。這表明從將作大匠這一中央官署控制下的製陶作坊內，亦抽調陶工參與了兵馬俑的製作。

“右”字類陶文在一號兵馬俑坑內發件兩件，一件爲“右”，一件爲“右亥”二字。“右”是“右司空”這一官署機構名的省文，“亥”是陶工名。“右”字類陶文在秦都城咸陽遺址及秦始皇陵出的磚瓦上發現很多，是秦代主要掌管燒造磚瓦的官署機構之一。由此可知“右司空”控制下的製陶作坊內的陶工，也參與了兵馬俑的製作。

3.來源於地方的陶工

秦始皇陵兵馬俑坑出土的陶俑身上，還發現一些在人名前冠一地名的陶工名。地名有咸陽、櫟陽、臨晉、安邑等，其中以帶有咸陽地名的陶文最多。目前已發現的陶文有：咸陽衣、咸陽危、咸陽野、咸陽賜、咸陽午、咸陽笥、咸陽高、咸陽秸、咸陽慶、咸陽木、咸陽文忌、咸處、咸嫘、咸行、咸路、咸翻、咸敬、咸稈、櫟陽重、臨晉茉、安邑口等，共二十一個陶工名。上述陶文中的咸處、咸行、咸敬……等，是省去了一個"陽"字，其全稱應是咸陽處、咸陽行、咸陽敬、咸陽路、咸陽嫘、咸陽翻、咸陽稈。上述二十一個陶工名前之所以都冠以地名，是表明這些工匠來源於何處。其中以來源於咸陽地區的人數最多。因爲咸陽是全國政治、經濟、文化的中心，製陶手工業比較發達，具有豐富經驗的優秀陶工比較多，因而從咸陽地區多徵調一些陶工參加兵馬俑的製作是必然的。目前僅發掘了兵馬俑坑很小的一部分，約占五分之一。待全面發掘後當會有更多的陶工名字發現。參加製作兵馬俑的陶工，可能不會僅限於咸陽、櫟陽、臨晉、安邑四地，也還可能有來源於其它地區的陶工名發現。

4.其它類陶工

兵馬俑坑出土的陶俑、陶馬身上的陶工名，凡在人名前沒有冠官署名和地名者，其來源於何處不明，暫列入其它類。此類人名多數僅有一字，少數爲二字。目前已發現的人名有：越悍、詠留、小速、次速、丁末、屈、田、王、武、安、北、其、冉、辰、中、文、尚、丙、胥、悲、眼、不、弋、止、山、杏、封、民、脾、鉼、棠、車、歬、捍、龠、申、甲、由、吳、示、禾、土、少、己、高、斗等，計四十六人。

以上四類總共有陶工名八十個。陶俑、陶馬身上爲什麼要打印或刻上製作者——陶工的名字？這是爲便於考核其製作陶俑、陶馬的數量和質量。《呂氏春秋·孟冬紀》記載："物勒工名，以考其誠。工有不當，以行其罪，以究其情"。這條資料清楚地說明物勒工匠名字的原因是便於考查其工作成績的好壞，如製作的成品質量不合格，要判其罪，追究其責任。在陶俑、陶馬身上留下工匠的名字，本來是秦政府控制和監督陶工的一種手段，但卻爲我們保留了一大批雕塑藝術匠師的名字。他們和秦俑這顆藝術明珠一起，將永載青史。

(二)中央和地方兩類陶工造型藝術風格的差異

上面介紹的四類陶工，其一、二類陶工來源於中央官署的製陶作坊；第三類來源於地方的民間製陶作坊；第四類陶工，其確切的來源雖難以肯定，但從其作品的藝術風格方面看，多數人當來源於地方，少數人來源於中央官署製陶作坊。總之，這些陶工大體可分爲來源於中央和地方兩大類。這兩類陶工製作陶俑的藝術風格表現出明顯的差異。

從體型方面觀察，來源於中央官署製陶作坊的陶工塑造的陶俑，其形體健壯，膀闊腰圓，立如鐵塔，穩定感和力感很強，有不可搖撼之勢。其所表現的氣質是剛毅、勇猛的力士形象。來源於地方民間製陶作坊的陶工塑造的陶俑，多數形體清秀，略有曲綫的旋律。有的寬肩細腰，衣的下襬呈大喇叭狀；有的形體修長，姿態瀟灑；有的形體瘦小，缺乏壯健感。和來源於中央官署製陶作坊的陶工塑造陶俑的雄健、剛直的風格適成鮮明的對比。

在陶俑的面形和神態的刻畫方面，來源於中央官署製陶作坊工匠的作品，多爲方形面龐，或長方形和圓形的面龐，粗眉大眼，闊口厚唇，寬額頭、高顴骨，是關中地區秦人的典型形象。所表現的人物性格多爲純樸、憨厚，神情肅穆，精神抖擻，好像是立於宮闕的衛士。來源於民間製陶作坊工匠的作品，其面形則多種多樣，有圓形、方形、長方形、漫長形、窄長形、上寬下狹形等等。面龐有的豐腴、結實，有的則較清瘦，有的修長。所刻畫人物的性格多種多樣，氣度不一。其風格使人感到親切、真實、活潑清新。

在技藝方面，來源於中央官署製陶作坊工匠的雕塑技藝，總的

說來比較熟練，水平較高。其所製作的陶俑的形體比例合宜，造型准確，解剖關系的處理也比較合理。焙燒的技術也比較高，俑的陶色多爲青灰色，火候均勻，質地堅硬。來源於民間製陶作坊工匠的技藝水平則參差不齊，有的水平較高，有的水平較差。其中雖有許多優秀作品，但也有些作品比較幼稚，比例失調。

來源不同的兩類陶工，製作陶俑的藝術風格有明顯差異。其差異產生的原因，是由於這兩類陶工生活經歷的不同，對生活體驗的差異和表現能力的高低不同，因而各自所創作的藝術形象必然不同。尤其在封建社會裏，手工業者的技藝是師徒相傳或父子相傳。技藝帶有一定的行會性、保守性，深受師承關係的影響。在同樣的主題和相同的題材下，不同處境和不同師承關係的作者會創作出不同藝術風格的藝術形象。

來源於中央官署製陶作坊的陶工，通過耳聞目睹，他們對駐扎在宮廷內外的衛士形象比較熟悉。守衛秦王朝宮闕的衛士是經過選拔的，都是體魄健壯，英姿勃勃，勇敢多力的戰士。這很自然地會被來源於中央官署製陶作坊的陶工選作塑造秦軍戰士的模特兒。因而他們所創作的秦俑形象，就像守衛宮廷的衛士一樣，立如鐵塔，威風凜凜。再者，這些工匠都在中央官署的制陶作坊內一起生活和從事生產勞動，在技藝上互相影響、互相學習，很自然地會形成共同的造型風格和藝術技巧。同時官署手工業管理制度比較嚴格，也決定了他們創作風格的嚴謹，一絲不苟。

來源於地方民間製陶作坊的陶工，他們日常生活所接觸的是廣大的社會羣衆。各種不同的形體、不同面容、不同性格的人物形象，是他們所熟悉和習見的。因而很自然地會把他們週圍所熟悉的人作爲塑造秦俑的模特兒。他們所攝取的人物形象的範圍更爲廣闊，更富有社會性。所以其塑造的秦俑形象更爲豐富多姿。另外，來源於地方民間制陶作坊的陶工，各人的師承關係不同，原來的技藝水平有高有低，因而表現在秦俑的雕塑水平方面也就參差不齊。

秦始皇陵兵馬俑這顆中國古代雕塑藝術史上的明珠，其製作者是從中央和民間制陶作坊中徵調來的一批陶工，他們是秦俑藝術的真正創造者。但陶工們製作秦俑是要根據一定的設計藍圖的。那麼秦俑製作藍圖的設計者是誰？文獻上沒有記載。但秦始皇陵園工程是由丞相李斯主持的。兵馬俑坑是秦始皇陵園建築的一部分，因而兵馬俑坑的設計，李斯等大臣似應參與其事。當然，俑坑的設計藍圖，必然要得到秦始皇的認可，體現秦始皇的意願和要求。我們在謳歌陶工們創造秦俑藝術的恢宏業績時，同時也應看到兵馬俑的設計者和主持者的作用。他們製定了秦陵兵馬俑的總構圖，規劃了秦俑創作的主題，又是秦俑制作的組織者和管理者。這種組織和管理是帶有強制性的，以至是很嚴酷的。這也就決定了秦俑藝術不同於古代西方的雕塑藝術。西方的雕塑藝術家能夠較多地反映作者的意念。而秦俑的作者則是奉命製作，個人的意念只能隱約地、曲折地反映。秦俑藝術所體現的是統治者的觀念，爲新興地主階級的利益服務的。

七　秦俑坑出土的兵器和製造工藝

秦始皇陵兵馬俑坑是座巨大的武器寶庫，現已出土金屬兵器三萬餘件。其中鐵兵器很少，基本上都是青銅製作的。有劍、戈、矛、戟、鈹、殳、鈹、弩機、箭鏃、彎刀等。劍、戈、矛、戟、鈹、弩機、鏃等幾種兵器，是人們常見的。彎刀、鈹、殳是比較罕見的兵器。

彎刀，通長65.2厘米，形如彎月，刀身兩面有刃，齊頭無鋒，斷面呈棗核形，是利用雙合範鑄後再經砥礪而成。這種兵器過去沒有到過。它沒有鋒不能當刺兵用，兩面有刃和形狀像月牙，說明它的使用方法是手握住柄運用肘部力量推、鈎兩用，是短距離格鬥的武器。根據《吳越春秋》記載，吳王"闔閭作金鈎"。此彎刀的原名應稱爲"金鈎"，後世稱之爲"吳鈎"。南北朝和隋唐時期的富家子弟把吳

鈎佩在腰間,作爲英俊威武的象徵,許多文人並採之入詩。如“驄馬金絡頭,錦帶佩吳鈎”(南朝鮑照《代結客少年場行》),“男兒何不帶吳鈎,收取關山五十州”(唐李賀《南園》第五首)。

鈹,這種兵器過去只從書上知道其名而沒有看到過實物。形狀和短劍完全相同,長30餘厘米,後端有個扁柱形的莖,插在一根長約3米的木柄上,作用像矛,是刺兵。《左傳·襄公十七年》記載:“使賊殺其宰華吳,賊六人,以鈹殺諸盧門”。可見春秋時已有這種兵器。當人們未見到鈹的木柄時容易誤認爲是劍,這也可能是過去罕見報道的原因吧!

殳,三號俑坑曾出土三十件。形狀呈圓筒狀,首呈多角尖錐狀,長10.5厘米,徑2.3厘米。出土時有三十件綑爲一束,並殘存有高約1米的木柄。《釋名》關於殳解釋說:“殳,殊也,長丈二尺,而無刃。”它是捶擊性的武器,不能用於鈎、刺、砍殺,適宜於作衛體用。原來是戰車上用的五兵(戈、矛、殳、鈹、弓)之一,後來漸漸變成儀衛的武器。宮廷的衛隊多執殳。如《韓子》記載:“楚國法,太子不得乘車至茅門。時大雨,王急召太子。廷中有水,太子遂驅車至茅門。廷尉舉殳擊馬,敗其駕。”三號俑坑內出土的兵器基本上都是“殳”,這也證明三號俑坑內的武士俑都是衛兵。

秦俑坑出土的兵器不但數量多,而且製作工藝先進,出土的青銅兵器都是鑄件。多用雙合範法鑄造。鑄出後再經銼磨、拋光。棱脊規整,刃鋒銳利,表面光潔度在6-8花之間,硬度爲HRb106度,約相當於中碳鋼調質後的硬度。經檢驗其合金的成分:青銅劍含銅爲71-74.6%,錫爲21.38-31%,鉛爲1.14-2.18%,其它還有微量的十二種稀有金屬。銅鈹,含銅80.11-83.06%,錫11.1-12.5%,鉛3.6-5.77%,鋅0.13%。銅矛,含銅量爲69.62%,錫30.38%。銅鐏,含銅量爲84.83%,錫15.15%。《考工記》說:“金有六齊(劑),六分其金而錫居一,謂之鍾鼎之齊(劑);五分其金而錫居一,謂之斧斤之齊(劑);四分其金而錫居一,謂之戈戟之齊(劑);叄分其金而錫居一,謂之大刃之齊(劑);五分其金而錫居二,謂之殺矢之齊(劑);金錫半,謂之鑒燧之齊(劑)。”錫含量的多少決定合金作成的器物組織細密的程度和硬度。俑坑兵器銅與錫的比例:劍爲3:1(弱),矛爲2.3:1(弱),鈹爲7:1(強),鐏爲5.6:1(弱)。與《考工記》比較,劍和矛的配比接近“大刃之齊(劑)”,鈹的配比與“削殺矢之齊(劑)”的配比相距較大。但鈹中含鉛的比例較大,鉛亦可提高鈹的硬度,反映了秦代已能按照武器性能的不同要求,制定一定的配比標準。實踐證明,青銅中含錫17—20%,最爲堅韌,錫佔30-40%時硬度最大,但易斷折。秦俑坑出土兵器的配比軟硬基本合宜。

值得特別注意的是,劍和鈹經電子探針及愛克斯熒光分析,發現其表面有一層致密的含鉻化合物的氧化層,厚度爲10-15微米。具有防腐抗銹的作用。因此埋在地下雖然經過兩千多年仍無銹,尤其是青銅劍表面還有亮光。這種工藝,歐美各國是近代才掌握的,而我國遠在秦代時即已能夠熟練地掌握了。不但秦俑坑青銅兵器表面有鉻化合物的存在,而且在西漢中山靖王劉勝墓中出土的銅鏃也發現有含鉻氧化物的存在。可見在兩千多年前的秦漢時期,這一先進的工藝已爲勞動人民熟練地掌握。這是冶金史上的一項奇蹟,是中國古代勞動人民對世界科學技術發明的又一偉大貢獻。

〈附注:本文是根據拙著《秦始皇陵兵馬俑》(中國旅遊出版社1983年版,文物出版社1983年版)、《秦陵兵馬俑的作者》(《文博》1986年4期)等文稿,綜合整理而成。〉

圖版目錄

THE TERRACOTTA ARMY OF EMPEROR QIN SHI HUANG

a great wonder in world civilization

The vaults housing the terracotta army of Emperor Qin Shi Huang (259-210 B.C.), located 1.5 kilometres east of his mausoleum in Lintong County, Shaanxi Province, are a group of three large attendant tombs, now numbered 1, 2 and 3, in the imperial necropolis. Vault 1 was discovered accidentally in 1974 when local peasants were sinking a well; Vaults 2 and 3 were brought to light in 1976 as a result of explorative drilling by the Qin Figure Archaeological Team.

All three vaults are huge in size, covering a combined area of over 20,000 square metres. Buried in them was treasure trove of rare and beautiful relics. Unearthed from the areas excavated so far are more than 30 wooden chariots, over 2,000 life-size pottery warriors and horses, and some 30,000 bronze weapons of various descriptions. Information already available indicates that the three vaults hold altogether 100 war chariots, 600 clay horses, nearly 7,000 pottery warriors and an armoury of bronze weapons which were used in actual battles.

The life-size terracotta warriors and horses are arrayed in ancient battle formation. The 6,000 found in Vault 1 stand in oblong formation as a composite force of war chariots and infantrymen. The 1,300 figures of Vault 2, in L-shaped battle formation, consist of war chariots, cavalrymen and foot soldiers. Vault 3, which houses a war chariot, 4 terracotta horses, and 68 warriors lined up along the walls as a guard of honour, is the supreme headquarters commanding the troops in Vaults 1 and 2.

The chariots and pottery figures are striking, with their life-like expressions. They epitomize the power of the armed forces of the state of Qin. They also provide vivid and tangible materials for the study of the accoutrements, military organization and battle arrays of the Qin Dynasty.

The Qin figures, with their varied colours and forms, give life and shape to varied personalities with distinctive traits. They display a natural, powerful and concise style producing irresistible charm. They represent a peak in the development of sculpture in ancient China, indicating that the art was quite mature and had formed a unique national style as early as Qin. In short, the Qin figures represent sculpture at the crucial stage of not only inheriting from the past but contributing to the legacy for the future. The figures are of epoch-making significance in the history of Chinese sculpture.

The discovery of the terracotta Qin army has aroused world-wide attention and been hailed as the "Eighth Wonder of the World" or "the most spectacular archaeological find in the 20th Century." Emperor Qin Shi Huang's mausoleum, including the vaults and the terracotta army, was listed in December 1987 among the world's cultural heritages by the United Nations Educational, Scientific and Cultural Organization (UNESCO), and has thus been officially granted its rightful position as one of the cultural wonders of the world.

I. THE IMPERIAL MAUSOLEUM AND TERRACOTTA ARMY

Qin Shi Huang*, the first emperor of the first feudal dynasty to unify China, was an outstanding statesman who made great contributions to the historical development of the country. Born in 259 B.C., he succeeded to the throne of the state of Qin in 246 B.C. at the age of only 13, so that state affairs fell into the hands of his ministers. After coronation at the age of 22, he took over the reins of government and, following the wishes of his ancestors, paid great attention to the development of agricultural production and also made it a point to reward military exploits. He soon turned Qin into a state of great prosperity and strength. He then launched the powerful military forces at his disposal into a series of wars, conquered the six other rival states (Han, Zhao, Wei, Yan, Chu and Qi) and succeeded by the year 221 B.C. in bringing to an end the state of separatist rule by contending principalities. He had succeeded in unifying the whole of China, and so established the Qin Dynasty. He proceeded to implement a series of measures to further consolidate the unification of the country, including standardizing the Chinese script, weights and measures, laws and monetary currency. His deeds had far-reaching bearing on later generations.

Emperor Qin Shi Huang toured his great empire many times to inspect the conditions of the people and to proclaim the civil and military achievements of his reign. It was on a tour of inspection in 210 B.C. that the emperor died at Pingtai in Shaqiu (in present-day Guangzong County, Hebei Province) at the age of 50. In September that year he was buried at the northern foot of Lishan Hill (east of present-day Lintong County, Shaanxi Province).

The emperor had had dreams of attaining immortality and sent Xu Fu and other alchemists across the East Sea to seek elixirs of eternal life, which, of course, did not exist except in the words of these fakes. Actually Qin Shi Huang knew very well that all men were mortal and he began having his mausoleum built immediately upon ascending the throne — a project which took 37 years to complete.

The great tomb of Qin Shi Huang looks like a large mound, or pyramid with its top cut off. The bottom of the tumulus is roughly a square, the top flat and spacious, accessible by means of two flights of steps half-way up a gentle slope. The mound, which originally stood 115 metres high and measured

---

*Qin Shi Huang, whose real name was Ying Zheng, has nearly always been referred to as such in Chinese literature even when mentioned in connection with events before he conferred on himself the title "Shi Huang" (First Emperor).

485 metres east to west and 515 metres north to south at the base, had been worn down by more than 2,000 years of rains and erosion to a height of 76 metres and a base size of 345 × 350 metres.

Beneath the tumulus is the burial chamber, which is surrounded by a clay wall. There are doors on all four sides of the wall; the main entrance, with five doors, is on the east side; the other three sides have a door each. The centre of the chamber is some 30 metres lower than the present ground level.

Lying in state in the chamber are the coffins of Emperor Qin Shi Huang and many precious funerary objects. According to *Historical Records* by the great Han Dynasty historian Sima Qian (2nd century B.C.), the burial chamber is a veritable underground palace of great magnificence filled with "strange and rare treasures." Its interior decorations include images of the sun, the moon and the constellations fixed on the ceiling and, on the floor, "rivers and seas of mercury." "Candles of fish grease were lit" to illuminate the inside permanently like daylight. To prevent theft of the rare treasures, "craftsmen were ordered to make and install mechanized crossbows, which would shoot automatically at anyone breaking in." It is hard to say how much credence one should give to these records, as the tomb has yet to be excavated, but the presence of mercury in the underground chamber has been scientifically ascertained. Tests made in 1981 and 1982 by the Physical Exploration Research Institute of the Academy of Geological Sciences showed strong indications of mercury at the centre of the underground palace over an area as large as 12,000 square metres. This would bear out the allegation that "rivers and seas were made of mercury."

Archaeological exploration has also revealed that the tomb of Qin Shi Huang used to be enclosed, on ground level, within an inner and an outer walled city, both oblong in shape. The inner city walls measured 1,355 metres north-south and 580 metres east-west, with a total circumference of 3,870 metres. The outer city was 2,165 metres north-south by 940 metres east-west, with a surrounding wall totalling 6,210 metres. Most of these walls, which were made of rammed earth, have collapsed, leaving only their foundations. However, a remnant each of the inner and outer walls on the southern side has remained, standing at about 2-3 metres high on a base 8 metres thick.

Gates were built in the walls — one on each side of the exterior and interior cities, except for the northern side of the interior city which had two gates. Every gate had its watch-tower. In addition, there was a tower at each of the four corners of the interior city. Various palatial buildings, such as halls serving as the living and sitting quarters of the imperial ghost, used to stand inside the interior city. Fires have long since reduced these buildings to piles of debris and burnt clay.

In an area of 56.25 square kilometres around Qin Shi Huang's tomb, repeated discoveries have been made over the years of important remains and relics. The part which has registered the greatest density of finds is an area of about 2 square kilometres inside the two cities and in their close vicinities. So far nearly 400 sites have been found of various descriptions, including attendant burial pits, attendant tombs and graves for the mausoleum builders. The whole necropolis, one could say, is a rich underground treasure house of cultural relics.

Among the important discoveries are the vaults housing the terracotta army, the pits in which the bronze chariots and horses were buried, the large pits holding the stables, 93 horseburial pits, another 31 containing meditating figurines. rare birds and animals, 45 attendant tombs, 103 graves for the

tomb builders, and various other pits serving as storehouses for the sepulchral palace.

It was a firm belief among ancient Chinese that there was life after death in the nether regions just as in the human world. The dead, therefore, were to be treated as the living. Emperor Qin Shi Huang was the supreme ruler in the human world and so he would remain among the dead. For this reason, his mausoleum with its mountain-like tumulus and underground palace was designed after the same layout as the Palace in Xianyang where he lived and reigned. The two enclosing walls symbolized the interior and exterior cities of his capital. He had in his lifetime large numbers of chariots, horses and guards for his tours and journeys, so chariots and horses, cast in bronze as funeral objects, were buried for his use in his afterlife. All ancient capitals had stables where fine horses were bred and kept for use by the court, so there were stable pits, large and small, in the grounds of the mausoleum to represent imperial stables. Likewise, the pits containing pottery birds and animals were meant to symbolize the imperial gardens and hunting grounds with their rare birds and animals, where the dead emperor might go hunting or otherwise enjoy himself. As for the host of chariots and troops, they represented the imperial garrison of the capital. In short, the Emperor had imitations made of everything he had in real life; the underground world was to be the replica of the empire he had ruled.

From the brief description of the layout of Qin Shi Huang's mausoleum and the intentions behind its designing, one can readily see that the terracotta army as an indispensable part of the whole project was highly significant. It was by means of a powerful army that the Emperor unified the whole of China, and was only natural that, fully aware of the importance of armed force, he had images made of his troops and had them buried near him to guard his ghost.

II. THE DISCOVERY OF THE VAULTS

The location of the vaults containing the terracotta warriors and horses — south of Xiyang Village to the east of Qin Shi Huang's mausoleum — was formerly a forest on sandy land strewn with countless tombs and prowled by wolves at night. Nobody had ever imagined that such bleak and desolate country would have buried underneath one of the greatest wonders in the history of world civilization — 8,000 troops and horses made of terracotta.

The story of the discovery goes back to March 1974. Local peasants including Yang Zhifa, Yang Pengyue and Yang Buzhi from Xiyang Village of Yanzhai Township, Lintong County, were sinking a well just south of their village. When they reached a depth of 2 metres, they came across some cakes of reddish burnt clay. When they dug on to a depth of 4.5 metres they found shards of pottery figures, bronze triggers of crossbows, bronze arrowheads and a brick-paved floor. Perplexed, they stopped digging and reported the strange findings to the Cultural Centre of Lintong County, which immediately sent people to collect specimens of the relics that had been unearthed. Close on their heels came leaders and archaeologists from the Cultural Relics Administrations of Shaanxi Province and of Beijing, who made on-the-spot inspection. They entrusted the provincial authorities of Shaanxi to organize a team of archaeologists for further exploration and excavation.

The author had the good fortune to serve as a member of

the team and was one of the first to start working at the site. Drawing upon previous experience, we at first thought the scale of the pit would not be very big, and it would probably take no more than 10 to 15 days to finish the entire excavation. But a great surprise was in store for us. After six months of exploration and trial digging, we found the pit, since named Vault 1, to be 230 metres long east to west and 62 metres wide north to south. It was 4.5 to 6.5 metres deep from the present ground level and covered an area of 14,260 square metres. Buried in it were as many as 6,000 life-size pottery warriors and horses. The massive terracotta army of such a large scale with so many figures had never been heard of by the archaeologists taking part in the project, although many of us had scores of years of experience in field and research work. It was also unprecedented in the history of archaeology whether in China or the world at large. Our excitement was extreme; no words could describe it.

The state paid great attention to this momentous discovery and, to ensure protection to the invaluable cultural heritage, in 1975 allocated a large amount of money to build an exhibition hall over the entire Vault 1 to protect the relics from the elements and also provide shelter for visitors viewing the wonder.

Construction of the hall began in 1976, and we archeologists focused our attention on surveying the area around Vault 1 in expectation of new finds. In the summer of 1976, a second vault of the terracotta army was discovered 20 metres north of the eastern end of Vault 1. The 5-metre deep L-shaped pit is 124 metres long from east to west and 98 meters wide (including the passages) from north to south, covering an area of 6,000 square metres. Trial digging indicated that buried in this vault were 89 wooden chariots and over 1,300 terracotta objects — including 470 horses for pulling the chariots and as steeds of the cavalrymen and over 900 life-size warriors.

Following Vault 2 closely, our drilling brought to light a third pit of the terracotta army to the north of the western part of Vault 1. This third vault is separated by 25 metres from Vault 1, and by 120 metres from Vault 2 at its eastern extremity. The plane figure of Vault 3 is in the form of the letter U, measuring 17.6 metres long from east to west and 21.4 metres wide from north to south. It has a depth of 5.2 to 5.4 metres and covers an area of 520 square metres. Inside the pit is a wooden chariot and 72 terracotta warriors and horses.

Our drilling also revealed a fourth pit at about 20 metres north of the middle part of Vault 1. It is 4.8 metres deep and rectangular in plane figure, measuring 48 metres east to west by 96 metres north to south and covering an area of 4,608 square metres. At the time of discovery the pit was filled with sand and silt, and no clay figures or other relics were found. This unfinished construction is attributed to the great peasant uprisings that took place toward the end of the Qin Dynasty that compelled the court to interrupt the work at the mausoleum and despatch the labourers to resist the insurrection. As no clay figures have been found in this pit, it is not counted in the vaults of the terracotta army. Generally, we speak only of the other three.

Following the completion of the exhibition hall over Vault 1 in May 1978, we began meticulous excavation of the pit. Up to the time of writing, from an area of 2,000 square metres we have unearthed 8 wooden war chariots, about 1,000 terracotta warriors and horses and 30,000 bronze weapons. Excavation is still going on in Vault 1.

A similar exhibition hall housing Vault 3 was completed in December 1988, with formal excavation and restoration of the figures for display scheduled for 1989.

An exhibition hall over Vault 2 was finished in 1990.

When the work at all three vaults is completed, the 8,000 terracotta men and horses will be drawn up in neat and awe-inspiring arrays to redisplay the formidable power and invincible might with which the Qin legions swept across China.

Visitors at the Qin vaults often ask the question whether the existence of such a massive number of terracotta figures has ever been recorded in history. *Historical Records, the History of the Han Dynasty* and a number of other ancient works give clear accounts of the construction of a mausoleum for Qin Shi Huang, but none about the vaults of the terracotta army. The only exception is a book entitled *Han Jiu Yi (Old Rites of the Han Dynasty)* which comes very close to mentioning the vaults in recounting the appointment by Emperor Qin Shi Huang of his Prime Minister Li Si to take charge of the building of his mausoleum. When the work was nearly finished, the book says, Li reported to the Emperor: "The 720,000 draftees and convicts working at Lishan (the mausoleum) under your servant's command have dug deep and reached the very bottom, which chisels can no longer penetrate and fire will not burn. Knocked, it sounds hollow as if the 'lower sky' is just underneath." Apparently, Li Si meant to say that the sepulchral palace had been made very deep and very large and its interior had been decorated like a world under heaven. The suggestion he wanted to convey was that the work might as well be brought to an end. Upon this, the Emperor is quoted as saying: "Extend sideways by another 300 *Zhang* (one *zhang* = 3.3 metres), and then stop." Actual surveys have shown that the vaults of the pottery army lie approximately within the stipulated radius and could very well have been part of the additional projects decided upon at the time of the above conversation.

There is also an interesting anecdote recorded in the work *Long Shang Ji* by Su Ting of the Tang Dynasty (618-907): "Xi Fang was to bury his deceased wife at her home in Lishan. It was a local custom that new tombs were built by levelling ancient ones. Xi destroyed an old mound and found below a grave of magnificent size and full of funerary objects. When it was opened, the sound of drums and horns was audible." The story gives no detailed description of the ancient tomb levelled, but the large number of funeral objects and the "sound of drums and horns" would seem to suggest symbolic description of a pottery army pit. Similar legends prevail among the local people to this day.

In the course of our work of exploration and excavation we came upon evidences that people must have seen the pottery figures before the year 1974. We found, for instance, tomb of the early Eastern Han Dynasty (first decades of the 1st century A.D.) built over Vault 2. Not only was its coffin pit dug right down to a group of pottery horses and cavalrymen but the latter appeared to have been damaged and moved. Obviously lived the earliest known discoverers of the pottery army as early as 1,800 years ago.

From the end of the 17th century the place was a public burial groud for the local people. Over Vault 1 alone there were more than a dozen tombs, all with their coffin pits dug down to the pottery figures.

In the course of our general survey local villagers recalled that their ancestors, when digging graves, had seen "monsters" which they could not name — certainly the same clay figures. He Wanchun, a septuagenarian, told us that when he was about

10 years old his father was sinking a well and found a "monster" the size of a man standing in the wall of the well. Water had shown at the bottom of the well, which after a few days suddenly dried up. Now we can be quite sure that there were crevices at the bottom through which the water seeped. But He Wanchun's father blamed the drying up on the monster, so he hoisted it up from the well and left it exposed to strong sunlight. Still there was no water. So he hung it from a tree and smashed it to bits.

Stories like these show that the buried terracotta warriors and horses have been stumbled upon from time to time. They did not arouse much attention simply because the people who saw them did not know what they were, or thought them evil and would only bring bad luck. They lay only about 5 metres below ground level, not any great depth. Certainly with the expansion of irrigation and water conservancy and with growing popular awareness of the importance of protecting cultural relics, their discovery was inevitable. It was only a matter of time.

III. THE STRUCTURE OF THE VAULTS

The three vaults of the sculptured ancient army constitute an underground architectural complex on a magnificent scale, a combined area of 20,780 square metres. The exhibition hall first opened to the public was the first to be built, that housing Vault 1. Its plane figure is rectangular with the longer side lying east-west. Leading down into the vault are five sloping doorways on each side. Those on the northern and southern sides, smaller in size (12 metres long by 1.6 to 4.8 metres wide), are the side entrances. Those on the eastern and western ends, larger in size (15 to 20 metres long by 3.8 to 6.6 metres wide), are the main entrances. Judging by the fact that the main array of pottery figures stand facing east, we know that Vault 1 itself also faced east and that the eastern entrances are the most important ones.

The space inside the vault is bordered by four corridors measuring respectively 60 by 3.45 metres on the eastern and western ends, and about 180 by 2 metres on the northern and southern sides. Inside the corridor-framed rectangle are 9 parallel trenches extending east-west, each about 180 metres long by 3.5 metres wide. They are separated from each other by partitioning walls of rammed earth. The floor of the vault is paved with blue brick, while overhead, the roof was built of timber covered with loess. The result has been a large wood-and-earth underground structure with trenches.

The entire vault must have been built in the following manner. First, an oblong pit was dug, then earthen partition walls running east to west were built in the pit. Wooden pillars were erected at intervals of 1.4 to 1.75 metres along the sides of the partition walls and the sides of the border walls of the pit. Beams were placed across the pillars. Thick roofing planks were laid in rows on the partition walls and beams, and the planks were covered with mats, reddish clay and yellow earth to form the roof of the vault.

The vault on completion stood more than 2 metres above ground level and, devoid of other brick or wooden structures, looked from a distance like an earthen terrace.

The vault measurement from ceiling to floor was 3.2

metres. After the human and horse figures were moved in through the doorways on the four sides, the doors were blocked with wooden posts and sealed with rammed earth, forming a closed, underground military barracks in which infantrymen stood guard along the side corridors while in the main trenches chariots were interposed among the foot soldiers.

Vault 2 is shaped like the letter L when viewed from the west with its eastern end on top. Access to the inside was by means of sloping doorways — four at the eastern end, five at the western end and two on the northern side. The vault faces east with the main entrances on the eastern side. The layout of Vault 2 is very complicated, but it may be roughly divided into four sections.

Section 1 or the eastern end of the pit, comparable in location to the top of the letter L, is edged on the four sides with corridors. In the middle are four parallel trenches stretching east and west and separated by partitioning walls. Arrayed inside are foot soldiers all holding crossbows obviously a formation of archers.

Section 2 refers to the right block of the whole vault, corresponding in position to the bottom of the letter L. It is bordered on the east and west by two north-south corridors, between which are eight trenches positioned east-west. Arrayed in the trenches, which are likewise separated by walls of rammed earth, are chariots exclusively, representing a formation of war vehicles.

Section 3, the middle of the letter L, adjoins Section 1 on the east and Sections 4 and 2 on the left and right. The western end protrudes from the letter L. Two partitioning walls extending east-west divide the space of this section into three trenches, in which are arrayed war chariots alternating with infantrymen. In the "protrusion" at the rear, however, are figures of cavalrymen only. Section 3 essentially represents an oblong formation of a mixed force composed of war chariots, infantry and cavalry.

Section 4 is the northern or left part of the east-facing pit, separated from Section 1 by a wall of rammed earth with a communicating door. This section, like Section 3, has two partitioning walls of rammed earth running east-west and dividing the space into three parallel trenches. Arrayed inside are pottery figures of men and horses to represent a cavalry unit.

The above sections are relatively independent of one another, but viewed together they form an organic whole.

The building procedure of Vault 2 was the same as Vault 1. First an L-shaped pit was dug in which partitioning walls were built to form the trenches. Wooden pillars were erected along the walls and the four sides of the pit to bear the beams fixed on top. Thick roofing planks were then closely arranged side by side on the beams and partitioning walls, and these were covered over by mats and loess in that order. The space inside was 3.2 metres from roof to floor, which was paved with brick. After the pottery figures had been moved in, the doorways were blocked with wooden posts and filled with rammed earth. In this way a closed, underground, L-shaped campsite was built.

Vault 3, shaped roughly like the letter U, also faces east, and has a sloping doorway on the east side. Immediately inside the door the visitor is greeted by a chariot and a team of four horses in a stable. To the right is a corridor leading to the north, flanked by two lines of terracotta warriors facing in as though on guard duty.

On the left of the corridor, lying lengthwise from east to west, is a spacious oblong hall lined on the sides with warrior figures, the floor strewn with remnants of deer antlers and animal bones.

It was the custom in ancient times that before a war was fought, sacrifices were offered to the gods for divine protection, and a rally of "war prayers" was held to raise the morale of the forces. The antlers and bones found here would indicate that the hall was intended as the site for such a ceremony of "war prayers."

Turning left from the stable, the visitor comes to another corridor leading south, likewise flanked by standing warriors facing inside. The middle of the corridor leads right (west) into a hallway and, further on, into a hall and a smaller rear chamber, all with warrior figures posted along the wall on guard duty.

The layout of the hall and the rear chamber suggests that the former was the place where the commander received his officers and handled military affairs, while the rear chamber was his bedroom.

Vault 3, like the other two, was a closed, underground wood-and-earth structure with trenches; its inside height was 3.6 metres. Its doorway was also closed by wooden posts and rammed earth after the pottery figures had been placed inside.

The three vaults together with the unfinished one formed a group of closely-knit underground structures. Vault 1 was meant to be the campsite or fort of the right legion, Vault 2 that of the left legion, the unfinished pit that of the middle legion, and Vault 3 the supreme headquarters of the imperial army. Together the four vaults formed a large-scale underground structure called in ancient times *bilei* or simply *bi* (fort or barracks with ramparts).

This term was used in an account of the battle of Changping fought in 260 B.C. between the states of Qin and Zhao. The two sides confronted each other in their positions behind ramparts *(bilei)*. General Lian Po of Zhao, aware of his inferior strength, simply hid behind the fortifications and avoided engagements in spite of repeated challenges from Qin.

Unable to provoke the Zhao into action, the Qin resorted to the stratagem of sowing discord. They spread the rumour that Lian Po was a far less formidable foe than Zhao Kuo, another general of the state of Zhao. The king of Zhao, taken in by this, appointed Zhao Kuo to replace Lian Po as his commander.

The next time the Qin advanced to provoke battle, Zhao Kuo led his troops out of the fortified camp to pursue and attack the enemy. He was not prepared for the large number of Qin who came out of ambush, cut into the Zhao camps and cut off their route of retreat. Four hundred thousand of the Zhao soldiers were thus wiped out.

The *bilei* was explained by Wei Liao, a military author in the middle of the Period of Warring States (475-211 B.C.), in his work *Wei Liao Zi*. Troops stationed in the ramparted fort, according to him, had strict boundaries between the units, which they could cross only under pain of death. The layout of the vaults for the Qin figures followed the same regulations, with strict lines of demarcation between the various legions and units to ensure a solemn atmosphere.

Vault 1, the diggings have revealed, caved in after it was set on fire. Vault 2 was partially burnt down, and the part untouched by fire also collapsed with the natural rotting of the wooden roof. Vault 3, which escaped burning, collapsed because of rotting, but before that happened, it had been broken into and its terracotta figures smashed. There have also been marks of human destruction that had taken place in Vault 1 before fire made it collapse — many weapons had been stolen and a number of human and horse figures reduced to bits.

As to the question who set fire to the vaults, conclusive evidence is still lacking. According to ancient works, however, after Xiang Yu (232-202 B.C.) crossed the Tongguan Pass in 207 B.C. at the head of his insurrectionary army, he set about "burning down his (Qin Shi Huang's) palaces, halls, mansions and barracks." These, we know, included the imperial Palace in Xianyang, the well-known Epang Palace and the buildings on the grounds of the Emperor's mausoleum. They might also have included the vaults of the terracotta army. This for the time being can only be a studied guess; further research is needed to find out what actually happened.

IV. SERVICE ARMS AND BATTLE ARRAYS

The state of Qin was a great military power reputed to possess a thousand war chariots, ten thousand war steeds, and over a million infantrymen. Relying on this formidable force, Qin Shi Huang crushed the six other states, accomplished the unification of China, and established the Qin Empire.

According to historical records the Qin military had four different service arms: war chariots, cavalry, infantry and navy. The first three arms were mainly employed in battles in the central and northern parts of the country, whereas the navy or water-borne force as chiefly used on the many waterways in South China.

However, there had been no detailed records concerning the various Qin forces, and over a long period of time their uniforms, weapons, equipment and battle arrays had remained largely unknown. The discovery of Qin Shi Huang's terracotta army has provided actual materials to answer these questions. Represented in the vaults are the three major arms, the navy being less important, and in such large numbers and with such vivid and colourful details that one might say one is witnessing the mightly Qin army itself.

A. WAR CHARIOTS, CAVALRY AND INFANTRY

1) WAR CHARIOTS

All the war chariots unearthed from the vaults of the terracotta army at Emperor Qin Shi Huang's mausoleum are made of wood and are of actual size. Remains of the chariots indicate that all of them had two wheels and a single shaft in the middle. The shaft, 3.7 - 3.96 metres long, is bent slightly upward in front, while the rear is fixed horizontally under the coach box. The coach box is oblong in shape, about 1.4 metres from side to side by 1.2 metres from back to front. It is surrounded on the four sides by lattice railings about 40 centimetres high. Getting on or off the chariot was via a door fixed at the back. The wheels are 1.35 metres high.

The fore end of the single shaft is attached to a cross bar, onto which double yokes are fixed to harness the horses.

Each wooden chariot is drawn by a team of four pottery horses, originally fully harnessed. They are of life size, about 2 metres long and 1.72 metres high at the head. The chariots are lacquered all over; some are also painted with elaborate designs and patterns. The horses are painted in a purplish red except for the manes and tails which are black and the hoofs which are white. All chariots and horses are fully equipped and harnessed presumably just as they were on the battlefield in their day.

The different costumes of the riders and the decoration of the chariots would make it appear that the chariots were of four different types: command chariot, spare chariot, chariot for four, and ordinary combat chariot.

① The Command Chariot

What distinguishes the command chariot from the other types is its magnificent decoration, consisting of exquisite geometric patterns painted on black ground colour over the body, and its round canopy. It is also decorated with a bell and a drum, which are not found on ordinary chariots.

There are three pottery figures aboard: the commanding general, the charioteer and the *che you* (literaly, "chariot right" or "right-hand man"). The three stand abreast: generally with the charioteer in the middle to drive; the general on his left to direct the movements of the troops by beating a drum or sounding a bell; and the "right-hand man" on the right, weapon in hand, to guard the commander and, if the chariot should be stuck, to get off and push it.

The three figures differ from one another in costume and pose. The general wears a purple or green outer garment over a red coat and is protected by a coloured suit of armour composed of small plates known as "fish scales." His shoes have square and upturned toes, and his cap resembles a kind of pheasant with its hackles raised in anger. A long sword at his side, he stands upright and imposing.

The charioteer is clad in a dark-brown suit of armour over a green long coat, and wears shin guards, shoes and a raised, "long cap." He is sculpted with arms stretched forward and hands clenched as if holding reins.

The "right-hand man" wears a red or green long coat, shin guards, a suit of armour and a raised, long cap. His left hand seems to have once held a sword, and his right arm bends forward in a gesture suggesting that it once held a long-handled weapon.

The bronze bell and drum on each command chariot are 27 centimetres high and bear exquisite patterns of stylized dragons and phoenixes. The drum, circular and flat, measures about 50 centimetres across; its circular side frame has three even-spaced bronze rings used for hanging it up.

In ancient China, gongs, drums, bells and banners were used to direct troops engaged in battle. To quote the ancient work *Wei Liao Zi* again, "The beating of the drum orders advance, heavy beating assault; the beating of the gong orders halt, heavy beating retreat; the bell is struck to transmit orders; the banners are waved to indicate directions of movement.... Death to him who beats the drum contrary to order, death to him who raises a hubbub, death to him who moves without being ordered by the gong, drum, bell or banner."

② The Spare Chariot

The spare chariot unearthed at the Qin tomb looks identical to the command chariot, except that it has no canopy, no bell or drum. While other types of chariots have three riders each, only two figures are found with the spare chariot: the charioteer and the "right-hand man." The charioteer, as the driver, occupies the middle of three positions, and the "right-hand man" as usual is on the right, leaving the left position vacant.

In ancient times the left was the side of honour. In the absence of the man held in respect, this position was to be left unoccupied. In a battle, the chariot used by the commanding general was called the principal chariot, which was as a rule followed by spare chariots. The *Book of Rites,* one of the Chinese classics, has a story about Duke Zhuang of the state of Lu when he personally led his forces in a battle fought at Shengqiu against the state of Song. His horses panicked and caused his defeat, and he fell off the principal chariot. He escaped capture by the enemy only because a spare chariot behind threw him a belt and helped him climb aboard.

The spare chariots unearthed at the Qin Mausoleum can be seen at the head of the cavalry columns in Vault 2. They were apparently for use by the cavalry commander.

③ The Chariot for Four

A chariot for four people has been discovered both in Vault 2 and Vault 3. The one in Vault 3, for example, has the same shape and structure as a command chariot complete with canopy, but there is no bell or drum. On board are four terracotta figures: a charioteer, an officer and two warriors in armour.

In costume and stance the charioteer looks the same as those on command chariots. The officer is clad in a long red garment and over it a breastplate with coloured patterns on the border. Wearing shin guards, shoes and a raised long, narrow cap, he has his left hand resting on a sword by his side; his right hand held something but it is difficult to tell what it was.

The two warriors are dressed alike: long coat, armour, shin guards, shoes, raised caps. They once held some weapon in their hands.

Ancient chariots normally carried three riders; it was rare to find four men on one vehicle. This number was an exception rather than the rule, since the extra man would add to the load and slow down the chariot, and being crowded together would handicap the warriors in brandishing their spears when engaged with the enemy.

The two four-men chariots, one each in Vault 2 and 3, were both found at the head of the columns. They appear therefore to be the leading chariots, or the vanguard of the wheel-borne troops leading the army on the march; in assault, they gave challenge and launched the first attack.

④ The Ordinary War Chariot

The ordinary chariot was meant for use by the rank-and-file warriors. It is also double-wheeled and single-shafted and pulled by a team of four, but devoid of canopy, bell or drum. There are three riders on each: a charioteer in the middle in charge of driving, flanked by two warriors to engage the enemy.

In both costume and posture the charioteers and warriors on ordinary chariots unearthed from Vault 2 look quite distinctive. The body of the charioteer is fully protected by a complete suit of armour, not only breastplate for the trunk, brassards and gauntlets for the arms and hands, but also gorget for the neck. His shins are protected and his head double-covered by a skullcap and a decorative raised cap. This outfit represents the heavy battle-dress of the time. This was necessary because the charioteer drove in standing position and was thus exposed to attacks by arrows. A wounded driver could cause the chariot to run out of control, leading to confusion and total defeat.

The two warriors are identically dressed: armour over long coat, shin guards, shoes and red skullcap. As to posture, the one on the right places his left foot a little forward, his left sleeve is rolled up to the elbow, one hand stretched as if keeping a tight grip on the reins, his right arm arches forward suggesting it originally held some long-shaft weapon. His head is turned slightly to the right, though he gazes straight forward. The warrior on the left stands identically but is an exact mirror-image of the first, forming with him a symmetrical pair. They seem to be gazing at each other in life-like intrepidity.

To be a charioteer, one had to undergo a strict course of training. Under Qin Dynasty law, if a trainee failed to master the art of driving at the end of four years' training, his coach would be subject to a heavy fine, he himself would be dismissed and forced to make up the four years' corvée from which he had been exempt. (See *Miscellany of Qin Code* based on unearthed Qin bamboo slips.)

The chariot warriors of Qin had also to pass screening by very exacting standards: "(He) must be below forty years of age, over seven *chi* five *cun* (= 1.73 metres) tall, fast enough to catch a galloping horse and, once mounted, able to make it vault and veer, rear and race all at will; he must also be able to wield a strong crossbow and shoot back and front, left and right, with flags or banners tied on him. Only when he has proved to be accomplished in all these can he be called a warrior of the chariot" (from *Liu Tao* or *Six Treatises on Strategy* written about the same time). This description fits very well the pottery images of the Qin chariot warriors. They all stand 1.80 metres or more, stalwart, dauntless statues of those who passed the test.

2) CAVALRY FIGURES

All the cavalry was unearthed from Vault 2, arrayed four horses in a group, three groups in a row. Altogether there are nine rows forming an oblong phalanx or cavalry column. The life-size horses measure about 2 metres long and 1.72 metres high at the head, their manes trimmed and tails plaited. On their backs they bear carved-on saddles, seemingly made of leather, bedecked with rows of studs and painted in red, white, blue and brown. The saddles, cushioned by blankets decorated with border tassels and coloured ribbons, are fastened on the horses by means of straps around the hindquarters at the back and on the sides by means of girths around the belly. No details of a horse known to the equestrian, such as halter, bridle with bit, and reins, are missing from the sculptured animal. The bridle bits are made of bronze, whereas the halters and reins consist of tiny stone tubes strung together with bronze wires.

In front of every horse stands a terracotta cavalryman in skullcap and knee-length garment with narrow sleeves. He wears a suit of armour reaching down to the waist only. Braced by a girdle and standing in riding boots, he has the reins of the horse in one hand and a bow in the other.

The war steeds and mounted warriors of Qin, according to the law of the time, must meet strict standards of selection. The horses must be 1.33 metres or taller, and must gallop, trot, rein up and rein in all according to order. Cavalry candidates were selected locally from among draftees. Both horses and men were subject to examinations after they reported for duty. If a horse was found to be sub-standard, the local officials of the county that sent it would be punished *(Miscellany of Qin Code)*. As for the men, according to the afore-mentioned *Liu Tao*, "cavalrymen must be under forty years of age and over 7 *chi* 5 *cun* (= 1.73 metres) in height. They must be of unusual strength and agility, able to gallop on horseback and shoot meanwhile left and right, forward and back with perfect ease. In pursuit of

the enemy they must be able to jump over trenches and moats, ride up hills and ridges, brave obstacles, ford marshes and throw great hordes into pandemonium. Only men like these can be called warriors on horseback."

The pottery war horses from the Qin Tomb vaults stand 1.72 metres high at the head, or 1.33 metres high from the withers. The correct way for measuring the height of a horse, either now or in ancient times, should be from the withers down, a more reliable point than the head. By this standard, the terracotta horse exactly satisfies the Qin Dynasty law.

The terracotta cavalrymen are no less than 1.8 metres tall; they look well-built, alert in expression, strong and spry. Typical images of mounted warriors of a crack force, they provide us with valuable and vivid material for the study of the Qin cavalry.

3) INFANTRY FIGURES

Of the terracotta warriors unearthed from the vaults, those of the infantry represent the largest number. They fall into two major categories — officers and men — and may be further subdivided into various types.

① Officers

The officers comprise three types: the general, the officer of intermediate rank and the subaltern. They are distinguished from one another mainly by the armour and caps they wear.

The general, as a rule, is clad in coloured "fish-scale" armour, a cap shaped like an angered pheasant and shoes with square and raised toes. With both hands in front of him as if once resting on a sword, he stands upright, solemn and imposing.

The costume for the officer of intermediate rank may be either of two types. One is clad in a Hun costume and a suit of armour with straight lower hems and a double-plate raised cap. The three officers of middle rank, for instance, found in the 4th, 8th and 10th trenches of Vault 1, are all in a style of Hun dress with tight sleeves, a suit of armour with straight hems in front and at the back, shin guards, army boots and double-plate caps. They stand serious and solemn, their hands apparently having held some weapon at one time. Another type is represented by the figures of the middle-ranking officers unearthed in Trench 2 of Vault 1 and in the fourth block of trial excavation of Vault 2. They wear a type of jacket with crossed lapels, the left lapel being folded over the right, a custom of the Han nationality. Their armour consists of only the breastplate in front, with nothing behind. It is tied on the body by means of two exquisitely designed belts forming a cross at the back. The rest of their garments are long trousers, shoes with square and upturned toes and double-plate raised caps. They stand with one hand resting on a sword and the other half-clenched as if holding some unidentifiable weapon.

Another middle-ranking officer dug out from the 4th trial excavation block of Vault 2 was found standing beside the figure of a general, looking respectful and cautious, obviously an aid-de-camp or some other subordinate to the general.

Terracotta figures representing junior subalterns have been excavated in much larger numbers and may be classified into two categories by their dress: those lightly dressed without armour and those heavily dressed with armour.

The differences that distinguish a subaltern from an ordinary warrior are: first, the former wears an officer's cap while the latter wears no cap; second, the warrior's armour consists of large but few plates whereas the subaltern's is composed of a much larger number of smaller plates.

The differences between the officers of intermediate rank and the subalterns are: first, the former wear caps with two raised decorative plates or boards whereas the latter's cap has only one raised board; second, the former wear armour with coloured borders, which are not found in the armour of the low-ranking officers.

An example is the figure of a subaltern of light battle-dress found in the southeastern corner of Vault 1. He is in a single-board officer's cap, a knee-high, girdled coat over a pair of short pants, showing his legs in puttees and his feet in shoes with square, upturned toes. His left hand appears to have once rested on a standing sword, his right hand once holding a spear or other long-shaft weapon. He stands firm and upright, looking invincible.

In contrast to the light-dressed subaltern, the heavy-armoured ones vary in costume detail. Normally they wear their armour over a long coat, but their legs are protected either in puttees or shin guards, and their feet in boots or shoes. Some hold bows, others hold spears or dagger-axes. They share one thing in common: all look strong and valiant.

② Warrior Figures

The Qin warrior figures, according to their costume, may be classified as of two types: the light-dressed ones with no armour and the heavy-dressed ones with armour. A figure of the former type wears a belted, knee-high coat over short breeches, legs in puttees and feet in army shoes of the time. Hair styled in a round bun topknot, he holds a crossbow or some long-handled weapon, perhaps a spear, halberd or battle-axe. Lightly dressed, this type of warriors can move with ease and agility and are deployed mostly at the fore of a battle formation. Of the 204 infantry figures that form the van in Vault 1, only three are armoured; all the rest are lightly dressed, without armour. This was because the vanguard had to be able to move quickly to catch the enemy off guard and deal him unexpected blows. This shows that as early as two thousand years ago military strategists were fully aware of the dialectical relationship between self-protection and attacking the enemy, between battle dress and combat requirements. That is to say, while outfits were meant for both self-protection and wiping out the enemy, priority in combat was to wipe out the enemy; the outfits had to be adapted mainly to destroying the enemy.

The armoured, heavy-dressed warrior figures are characterized by their suits of armour over knee-high coats, breeches, shin guards or leggings, shoes or army boots. Some carry bows or crossbows, others hold long weapons like dagger-axes, spears or halberds. Their hairstyles were round or flat buns made up of six plaits. Some have their hair covered by cone-shaped skullcaps.

So far no helmets have been found on any of the warrior figures. It is recorded in historical documents that the Qin troops did have helmets but that they were so fearless that they did not wear them in battle. The absence of helmets from the vaults seems to confirm this dauntless spirit.

B. ARRAY OF CHARIOTS, CAVALRY AND INFANTRY

It was already known to ancient Chinese strategists that an army could fight with combat effectiveness only when they were in a certain formation or battle array. According to *Liu*

Tao or *Six Treatises on Strategy,* if the troops were to fight individually, "a lone mounted soldier would be no match for one footman;" well-arrayed in battle, however, "one mounted soldier would be a match for eight footmen." The same idea has been fully shared by Friedrich Engels when he stressed the great importance of combat formation for cavalry.

An armed force is not a martial arts troupe, it must rank battle formation above individual skills in importance. Ancient troops, therefore, were maintained in certain patterns of formation whether they were engaged in field operations, in the siege of a city or in pursuit of an enemy. "Individually," says Sun Zi in his *Art of War,* "the courageous should not advance, nor the timid retreat." Anyone who dared to break ranks would be punished by military law.

King Wu (c. 11th century B.C.), founder of the Zhou Dynasty, on his famous expedition against the tyrannic last king of Yin, issued an order that each soldier in combat, after charging the enemy and advancing a few steps, must look round to adjust his position so that the battle formation be kept throughout the engagement.

Examples abound in history, in which strict battle arrays, or the lack of them, decided the outcome of an engagement. At the Battle of Yanling (575 B.C.), the army of Chu was defeated because it "was not in orderly array." At a battle fought on the River Bi, when the Jin army was doomed to a débâcle, one of its legions maintained its formation and was able to retreat in good order, while the others suffered total destruction because they broke ranks.

Great soldiers in ancient times, therefore, are known to have attached great importance to the disposition of the troops in definite arrays. Yet, owing to the paucity of concrete descriptions in extant ancient literature, the composition of these battle arrays had remained a total riddle until the discovery of the Qin figures.

Qin Shi Huang's terracotta army has presented the ancient battle formations in a way not only true-to-life; they are also almost "as large as life." The riddle of how ancient armies were arrayed in battle has been solved.

1) BATTLE ARRAY IN VAULT 1

There are about 6,000 terracotta warriors and horses in Vault 1. At the time of writing, however, only some thousand warriors, eight war chariots and thirty-two horses have been excavated. The following is the way they are arrayed.

The chariots are arranged in mixed compositions with the foot soldiers, composing a rectangular formaton facing east. It consists of four parts: the van, the rearguard, the main body and the flanks.

The vanguard is formed by three ranks of warriors, all facing east; with 68 men in each rank. It has a total strength of 204.

Immediately behind the van is the main body of the formation, a massive array extending about 184 metres with war chariots interposed with infantrymen in close order.

On either side of the main body is a single rank of men extending also for 184 metres. They stand facing out (to the north and south) and are the side guard of the formation.

At the end of the main column to the west are another three ranks of soldiers, of whom two rows stand facing east, while the third row faces west to guard against attacks from the rear.

The above goes to show how compactly the array of the pottery army is organized.

An important principle followed in ancient times in lining

up a battle array was that each formation must have a crack force as the van and a powerful force to bring up the rear. Without a dauntless vanguard, the army would be like a sword with no edge; without a forceful rearguard, it would be like a sword with no hilt. Only "with a sharp van and a protective rear," says Sun Bin (c. 4th to 3rd century B.C.) in his *Art of War*, can an armed force "hold its own and repulse the enemy." The battle formation of the terracotta Qin army conforms with this principle.

The pottery warriors in the van of Vault 1 are light-dressed without armour or helmet. They have their hair tied up in buns and legs protected in leggings, and use bows or crossbows as their weapons. They can only be the fleet-footed warriors who could "scale great heights and march long distances."

Behind the van is a column of 38 files composed of chariots and foot soldiers. All the warriors, being the heavy-dressed ones, wear armour and shin guards and hold a variety of long-shaft and shooting weapons. They are outfitted for protracted hand-to-hand encounters with the enemy.

The battle formation in Vault 1 clearly places the light and vigorous force in front, followed by the heavy and powerful, to integrate assaulting impact with enduring strength. This created a mighty fighting force with which to shatter enemy positions and wipe out a strong foe.

The war chariots at the eastern end of Vault 1 are positioned in pairs, each pair a fighting unit. One of the pair is the leader, the other the supporting chariot. In defence the two would cover each other in attacks from all sides; in assault they would mount a pincer movement. The two were inseparable; separated, both would be doomed to failure.

As for coordination between chariots and men, each chariot is manned by three armoured soldiers, namely one charioteer and two warriors, and is covered by infantrymen on all sides. Twelve men precede it in three rows of four, forming a squad to fight the enemy in front. Flanking it, soldiers varying in number between 52 and 60, also in ranks of four, form two small phalanxes to march alongside the chariot, each responsible for dealing with the enemy from one side. Then a fourth group of between seventy-two and over a hundred men bring up the rear of each chariot.

This system of grouping four bodies of foot soldiers round a chariot, called the "five-element formation" in its time, was meant to ensure close coordination between the two arms and to provide greater infantry cover to the chariots. It also allowed ample room for the employment of flexiable tactics. When the chariots were handicapped in movements in defensive operations or on rugged terrain, greater reliance was placed on the infantry. On flat terrain the chariots were placed ahead of the foot soldiers and employed as the main combat force assisted by the infantrymen. This tactic is summarised succinctly by an ancient writer in these words: "Chariots precede the foot, with the latter filling up the gaps, ... Despatch chariots to meet the enemy; follow up with the soldiers to meet the changing situation." (*Research in a Mountain Cottage: Chairot Warfare.*) It appears clear, therefore, that the relative positioning of the chariots and foot soldiers changed with varying topography and combat situation.

2) BATTLE ARRAY IN VAULT 2

The general layout of the soldiers in Vault 2, as explained before, is like a thick letter L, and consists of four small phalanxes.

Phalanx 1, situated at the top of the L, forms the front corner of the whole formation. It is composed of two parts: the borders and the core. Standing all along the four sides are 174 figures of bowmen, lightly clad without armour. They surround the core of the formation, which is a group of 160 archers arrayed in eight files of 20 men each. All covered by armour, they are the heavy-dressed type and hold bows and crossbows as their weapons.

Why is it that the figures on the four sides are standing while those in the middle are squatting? Two rules were to be observed in ancient times by troops using shooting weapons. First, no fellow soldiers must stand in front of those shooting so that nobody of the same side got hurt; second, archers of the same unit must take turns at shooting to keep arrows flying at the enemy and give him no reprieve. The two groups of archer figures in this phalanx are supposed to alternate between the postures of standing and squatting, depending on whether or not it is their turn to shoot. That is to say, the archers on the sides shoot first at the enemy and then squat down; they are followed by those in the middle, who stand up to start shooting. The two groups take turns at shooting so that continuous flights of arrows keep the enemy at bay.

Phalanx 2, to the right of the base of the L-formation is a chariot array composed of eight lines of eight chariots each, sixty-four in all. Each chariot, drawn by a team of four, carries three armoured figures — a driver and two warriors. There are no foot soldiers attached to it on any side, a type of troop deployment different from the practice prevalent in the Yin and Zhou dynasties (c. 16th to 11th century B.C.) or the Spring and Autumn Period (770-476 B.C.) when chariots were without exception supported by infantry. This new discovery has revealed something we did not know before. The change must have followed the development of foot soldiers during the Warring States Period (475-221 B.C.) into an independent infantry arm. Battles were now fought by coordinated action between units of horse, foot and chariot, and it was presumably no longer necessary for each individual chariot to have foot soldiers assigned to it.

Phalanx 3, the middle of the L-formation, consists of three files of chariots reinforced with horse and foot. There are six chariots each in two of the files, and seven in the middle file, totaling nineteen. Each carries three occupants, namely one driver and two fighters as usual. At the very end of the left file a chariot with the figure of a general is the command chariot, which is followed by a group of infantry. Of the other chariots, those in front are followed by eight infantrymen each and those toward the back are supported from behind by a group of 28 or 32 foot soldiers. The rear of the phalanx includes two groups of cavalrymen, with four horses to each group, plus 32 infantrymen arranged in eight ranks of four men each. It forms an oblong echelon behind the last war chariot.

The presence of mounted soldiers in the composition of ancient battle arrays is also a new element that has just come to light. The cavalry was quick and mobile and could be used as a reserve strike force giving greater flexibility to the chariot formation.

Phalanx 4, an array mainly of mounted soldiers, occupies the corner of the letter L. A long rectangle of three columns consisting of six chariots and 108 horses and men, it may be divided into two parts: the van and the body. Forming the van or the phalanx head are the six chariots, two in each column, one behind the other but separated by a row of mounted soldiers between each two chariots. Each has two riders: a driver and a warrior. Cavalrymen sandwiched between the chariots are in rows of four, making a total of twelve mounted men. The body of the phalanx is composed of 96 cavalrymen, who stand with their steeds in rows of four in the three columns. Altogether in this phalanx are 108 horses, each with the figure of its rider standing by holding the reins.

The four phalanxes described above form an organic major formation. This form of troop deployment has been described in ancient books on the art of war as: a major formation comprises minor ones, a large battle-array consists of smaller ones, with each part linked to another, every section covering all the others. Unless a large array comprises several small ones, it would be handicapped in flexibility, and "would not be able to break into smaller fighting units" to adapt to complicated terrain or the ever-changing enemy situation: the troops would find themselves unable to spread out or take different positions, or even be thrown into confusion, crowding and jostling against each other.

The positioning of the four phalanxes reflects well-conceived military thinking. The archers' phalanx, protruding in front, faces the enemy on three sides— the front and the two flanks — and is a position to give full play to the power of their bows and arrows. The chariot formation, on the right, can engage the enemy in front and from the right and, availing itself of the "arrow cover" from the archers, is ever ready for both offensive and defensive actions. The cavalry, on the left and facing the enemy only from one flank, is covered on three sides in defence while retaining complete freedom to disengage itself from the main body in an assault. The mixed phalanx of foot, horse and chariot, placed in the middle of the formation, serves as the central coordinating force to link up the other three phalanxes described above and the rearguard placed behind. All five units, offering support to one another, may break up into separate combat units or combine to fight as an integral whole of multiple arms. Highly manoeuvrable, the battle-array under the command of a seasoned commander could perform miraculously on the battlefield.

The mixed composition of foot, horse and chariot in the same formation represented an important change taking place during the Warring States Period (475-221 B.C.). Before that a battle-array meant an array of chariots. The change came about with the infantry and cavalry becoming independent arms of the forces.

The three arms were meant to serve different purposes. The chariots were to "storm strong fortifications, put the formidable enemy to rout, and block the fleeing foe." The cavalry, being mobile fighters, were to "chase the foe in flight, disrupt his routes of food supply, and attack lightly armed marauders." Foot soldiers, on their part, would be employed mainly in operations in closed or marshy terrains, where the manoeuvres of chariots and horses became difficult, or on garrison duty at forts and passes.

Sun Bin, an eminent military writer quoted above, wrote in his *Art of War: Eight Arrays:* "Chariot, horse and foot are to be organized in three arrays and positioned one on the right, one on the left and one in the middle. When the terrain is favourable, chariots should be largely employed. When it is difficult, horses should be largely employed. In distress, arrows should be resorted to." In other words, according to Sun Bin, topography and combat situation must be taken as the determinant factors in deciding which of the arms should be used as the main force and which as the auxiliary force. Only a good coordination of the three arms could ensure victory.

A brilliant example of this was the Battle of Changping

fought in 260 B.C. between the states of Qin and Zhao. The Qin feigned defeat and began to fall back, inducing the unsuspecting Zhao to pursue them. They then unleashed a force which they had laid in ambush to cut off the retreat route of the Zhao. Meanwhile a Qin cavalry unit 5,000 strong struck between the various camps of the Zhao, encircling them in separate pockets. Thanks to the well-coordinated use of the three arms, Qin wiped out four hundred and fifty thousand of the enemy, entering a famous battle into the pages of history of ancient Chinese warfare.

3) BATTLE ARRAY IN VAULT 3

Vault 3, the command headquarters, has yielded sixty-eight warriors as well as a chariot harnessed to the figures of a team of four horses. The warrior figures are placed as follows:

4 standing behind the chariot: a driver, two armoured warriors and an officer;
22 in the northern hall, lined on the sides, with 11 in a line;
8 in the corridor leading south;
6 in the hallway on the south side;
24 in the front hall; and
4 in the rear chamber.

All the figures line the sides with their backs to the wall. This evidently is no battle array but a line of guards. Furthermore, the arms held by them are *shu,* ceremonial weapons used more for defense than offense. All signs indicate the warriors in Vault 3 are members of a bodyguard.

The three vaults are not isolated from one another, but are the organic, component parts of a major military formation. Vault 1 represents the legion on the right, Vault 2 that on the left, and the unfinished vault mentioned above represents the legion in the middle. Vault 3 is the supreme headquarters in over-all command. The terracotta army, with its full-scale units and arrays, may be regarded as a life-like reproduction of the Qin army, a graphic diagram of ancient battle formations, a living textbook on the art of war. It is of incomparable value in the history of military affairs.

V. THE QIN FIGURES AS WORKS OF ART

The Qin Tomb figures have become the focus of attention not only because of their great numbers and life size. They also give food for thought and arouse enduring fascination especially with the vivid images, the lucid and concise style and the superb craftsmanship they display.

The Qin figures are works of a mature classical art, which carried forward the good traditions of pre-Qin sculpture and brought it to heights never before attained. They ushered in a new period of further development. The art as represented by the terracotta figures was a model for posterity and, as a connecting link between the past and the future, was of epoch-making significance in the history of Chinese sculpture.

A. REALISM IN THE QIN SCULPTURAL ART

The Qin figures have attracted widespread fascination and won sincere praise for their "eternal charm," having truthfully mirrored social life as it was and faithfully representing the images of the Qin legions in their thousands — images, as it were, of flesh and blood, of feeling and character, not just a group of artificial, lifeless idols.

The Qin warrior figures show distinctive individual personalities just as they are different in facial expression with no two among the thousands looking alike. The face, for instance, with the broad forehead, high cheekbones, thick brows, large eyes and stiff beard is the face of a hardy and fearless man. The round face with regular features reveals a frank and openhearted character. The oval face with fine features shows a genteel disposition. Then there is the square face with honest simplicity clearly written on it. Some with protruding brows and piercing eyes seem to display unrivalled bravery; others glowering with knitted brows appear to be bursting with indignation, while still others portray an alert personality with their handsome brows, clear eyes and well-groomed, pointed "imperial" moustaches.

The figures also depict warriors of different age groups and are therefore different in appearance and expression. Generally, the older soldiers with lined foreheads appear to be sedate and serious as weather-beaten veterans who have seen much of the world. The young soldiers, on the other hand, generally have chubby faces, smiling with naivety.

The success of the art of the Qin terracotta figures lies also in the characterization of various differing types in military status and occupation, including senior, intermediate and junior officers as well as soldiers of various arms and duties.

The figures of the generals are distinguished without exception by a stalwart stature and elaborate attire. They wear double coats, one beneath the other, coloured armour of "fish-scale" pattern, shoes with upturned toes and pheasant-shaped caps. They are marked with an air of eminence.

But they all show individuality. One wears signs of nobility in his fine features and long beard; he is sculpted with the right thumb touching the neighbouring index finger, a detail in Chinese gesture that helps depict a resourceful mind at the command of a great army. Another general, one with a whiskered face who stands with both hands resting on a sword and with head held high, looks the epitome of awe-inspiring power. One can imagine the resolute bearing with which he stands on the battlefield as he orders his legions to charge the enemy. There is also one with large features and broad cheek bones, his forehead marked by arched lines indicating rich experience in numerous campaigns.

The task of a general lay in directing his legions to victory, not in personal prowess or individual bravery. Qin law stipulated that if a commanding general personally charged forward at an enemy van he would be committing an offense punishable by exile. That is why the generals unearthed from the Qin vaults carry no other weapon than a double-edged sword, a light arm for personal protection only. In bearing, however, they all show themselves to be well-tested strategists, resourceful, resolute, knowledgeable about their own men and enemy conditions and, therefore, fully confident as to the outcome of a battle.

Officers of intermediate rank are all dressed in long coats, covered by a breastplate or a waist-length suit of armour with patterned borders, and an officer's cap on the head. They are distinguished from the rank and file not only by their dress but also by the posture and comportment in which they carry themselves. One who stands beside a general and looks serious and respectful is apparently a senior aide-de-camp. Another officer of great height and solemn mein appears distinctive with an "imperial" moustache and knitted brows; he is portrayed as a man of resolution and confidence. With a sword in his left hand and what appears to have been a drum stick in his right, he

seems to be waiting for an order before he starts beating the drum for the troops to move forward. Bells and drums, as we have discussed, were used to direct battle movements: the battalions would "advance when the drum is struck, and charge at the enemy when the drum is belaboured." If the sound of the drum became a thunderous roll, the legions would brave the flights of arrows and the rain of spears and fall on the enemy wave upon wave.

Figures of junior officers are too numerous to be described individually; so only a few examples are presented here.

There are two figures at the eastern end of Vault 1 that look different from the rest of the 200-odd warriors forming the vanguard. One of them, standing 1.97 metres tall at the left end of the vanguard formation, of broad shoulders and solid build, wears armour and an officer's cap. He seems to have once held a sword in his left hand and a lance or some other long-shaft weapon in the right. Erect and dauntless he stands, with lips pursed and eyes fixed like a man of iron will. Yet the serious and respectful caution, which is also written on his face, places him in the bracket of subalterns, one devoted to duty. His colleague, who stands near the right end of the formation, wears an officer's cap too, but no armour, being a light-clad fighter. Holding similar arms (seemingly a sword in the left hand and a long-shaft weapon in the right), he stands with belly bulging and head raised, a posture which accentuates his courage, giving him the convincing image of a warrior who, in the thick of the fight, would not fail to place himself ahead of his men.

The stances assumed by the men of different branches of the army are largely decided by their respective duties. An example in point is the group of three figures excavated from trial block No. 1 of Vault 2. They were found standing abreast behind their chariot, with the driver in the middle and a warrior on either side. The driver is sculpted with the upper part of the body leaning slightly forward and both arms stretched in front, his hands half clenched as if still holding the reins. Looking serious and attentive, he has his eyes riveted, as it were, on the team of four drawing the chariot. The warrior on the left is "standing at ease" with his right foot a half step forward, his left hand holding some long-shaft weapon. The sleeve of his right arm is rolled up to the elbow, his right hand appears to be resting on some part of the chariot to hold himself steady. With his head turned slightly to the right, he is all ears to the orders that may be given from time to tme. His comrade-in-arms, on the right, is in every way his mirror image — left foot out, right hand holding a weapon, left sleeve rolled up, left hand resting on the chariot, and head turned slightly to the left at attention. The four horses in front have their heads raised, mouths open in an unheard neigh, and hoofs about to gallop. The horses restive, the driver trying to hold them back and the warriors all ears for orders conjure up a battlefield scene in which the chariots are harnessed, the fighters waiting for the word to jump aboard and the driver ready to crack the whip and drive forward to meet the enemy. The great unknown artists of Qin successfully organized the human and animal figures into a harmonious whole, cleverly coordinating their postures and expressions, portraying action through still images, and guiding the viewers' vision out of a limited space far afield into a vast battleground.

The phalanx of archers and crossbowmen at the eastern end of Vault 2 consists of figures in two postures — standing and kneeling. The men standing on the borders of the formation, 174 in number, are all realistically and vividly modelled in light battle-dress. Their feet are planted apart with the left one slightly in front, at a T angle with the right one. Their left leg is a little bent and the right one straight and taut. The body turned slightly to the left, each one has his left arm stretched forward and the right bent before the chest. With eyes fixed forward and lips pursed, as though in silent exertion, the group is perhaps engaged in archery exercises.

The way they hold themselves reminds one of a passage in *Chronicles of Wu and Yue* in which Chen Yin explained to the King of Yue the art of archery:

> The correct way of shooting, to the best of your servant's knowledge, is to put the left foot a little forward, forming a right angle with the right foot which remains at the back. One should imagine a branch is held in the left hand and a baby in the right arm. Let the right hand release the bowstring without being aware of it. And that, Your Majesty, sums up the way of shooting with a bow.

Here, the enigmatic phrase "release the bowstring without being aware of it" means that the archer's eyes should always be fixed on the target and not directed back to his own right hand.

The archer figures at Qin Shi Huang's tomb are doing exactly as ancient writers directed, and are sculpted according to the way bowmen of old were supposed to shoot. There they stand before us, a company of men seemingly in the flesh, conscientiously training in the art of archery. We feast our eyes on them both as beautiful works of art and as models that provide us with information about the art of war in ancient times.

In the middle of the phalanx are 160 armoured or heavy-arrayed bowmen, all in kneeling posture, that is, with the left leg bent and the right knee touching the ground. The right arm hangs in a curve at the side and the left arm is bent over and held in front of the chest. Apparently a bow was once held in the two hands, the left one high over the right. The body is slightly turned to the left and the eyes, on the alert, gaze ahead.

At the right-hand corner in the rear of the phalanx stand, side by side the figures of a general and his aide-de-camp, both with legs planted apart and eyes sweeping the front. The grave look of their piercing eyes seems to radiate invisible threads which weave and string through the actions and expressions of the 300-odd men and hold the phalanx together as a living whole. And by following these threads one sees a unit of the Qin army performing, on orders, varying parades — changing, as an ancient writer puts it, "from round to square array, from sitting to standing posture, from march to halt, from left to right, from front to rear, from skirmish to close order, and from concentration to dispersal." When each soldier is studied alone, it can also be seen that he is going through individual training in the essentials of archery. The whole group, therefore, presents a true-to-life, dramatic and elucidating scene of military drills more than 2,000 years ago.

The scene reminds one of a story of Sun Wu, an ancient strategist who lived in the 6th century B.C., popularly referred to as Sun Zi or Master Sun. One day, Helu the King of Wu wanted to see how he trained troops. He asked Master Sun to try his training method on 188 beauties he had selected from among his palace maids. Sun proceeded to divide the girls into two formation, each captained by a favourite concubine of the King's. He ordered the girls to hold halberds in their hands, and asked:

"You all know on which sides your hearts and backs, left and right hands are?"

"Yes," the young women replied.

"When I say front," Master Sun continued, "I mean the direction your heart faces. When I say back, I mean the direction behind your back. When I say left or right, I mean the side of your left or right hand."

The girls again said, "Understood."

After giving the necessary explanations of his orders, Sun struck the drum to order a right turn. The young women burst out giggling.

"There is a lack of strict discipline and of clear explanations," Sun said, "That is the fault of the commander." He then went on to explain his instructions repeatedly.

After that, he struck the drum to order a left face, and the women burst out giggling again.

"The commander should be held responsible for the lack of discipline and of clear explanation of his orders," Sun repeated. "But when the orders have been fully explained and yet still they are not carried out, it becomes the fault of the subalterns." Thereupon, he ordered the beheading of the leaders of the left and right formations.

Alarmed at the peril facing his beloved concubines, the King on the rostrum, trying to overrule his order, said, "Without these two consorts I would lose all interest in life. I beg you not to execute them."

"Your liege has been appointed the commanding general." replied Sun," and when he is with the army, a commanding general may override orders from his sovereign."

He had the two team leaders beheaded, and appointed their deputies to succeed them as leaders.

When he struck the drum again, all the women in the formations acted in strict accordance with the orders given — turning left and right, front and back, sitting, kneeling or standing — without the slightest noise.

The master then sent a courier to the rostrum to report to the King: "The troops have been trained, ready for Your Majesty to come down for a close inspection. You may employ them anywhere, to the extent of sending them through fire or flood."

Great soldiers of ancient times attached vital importance to troop training. The "Combined Biographies of Yuan Ang and Chao Cuo" in *History of the Han Dynasty* has the following passage on this subject:

> Unless carefully selected and strictly drilled, the troops will fail to keep precise time in camp life or coordinate their actions with exactitude; they will not know how to exploit favourable conditions or avoid unfavourable ones; they will quail before an attacking enemy and go out of step with the directions of the drum and gong. These failings can only stem from the lack of strict drilling. Pitted against an enemy, a hundred of such troops would not be equal to his ten.

But this description does not apply to the troops of the state of Qin. When General Wang Jian led 600,000 of them in a massive campaign against the state of Chu, instead of throwing them in an immediate offensive, he spent time first in training them and consolidating their organization. When eventually they were plunged into the fight, a great victory was won.

The formation of the bowmen just described a few paragraphs back reflects exactly the thinking behind the strictness with which the Qin army was drilled and disciplined. The 300 archers, acting as one man according to orders, each one so resolute and brimming with vim and vigour, can only be the kind of crack force which would not hesitate to go "through fire and flood" at the sound of the drum.

While the Qin tomb figures are characterized by a clear

individuality which marks different characters, expressions and occupations, it is not difficult to discern the trait that they all share in common — the quality of being "brave in national warfare but timid in personal fights," a quality essential to an invincible army. The figures are also a reflection in sculpture of the spirit underlying the mental outlook of a new landlord class which had just begun its ascent in history. Not only are they true-to-life models of a powerful ancient army; they stand for the spirit of an era, the portrayal of an important period of history. In this sense, they have a place of great prominence among the most outstanding works of realistic sculpture handed down from ancient times.

B. VIGOROUS STYLE AND SUPERB ARTISTRY

The art as represented by the Qin tomb figures is different from Western sculpture in that it is implicit in expression and introvert in feeling; it emphasizes the revelation of the subjects' inner world through their facial expressions and in a simple and vigorous style characterized by a powerful internal force.

To be specific, the art of the Qin figures is distinguished by the following features:

First, in subject matter and general layout, the figures were meant to represent a powerful army complete with three legions and in all its magnificence. Other ancient sculptures taking the army as theme have been discovered, but none of them, Chinse or foreign, can compare with the Qin figures in size and number. With warriors and horses literally by the thousand, the Qin figures are set apart from all others by the imposing sight they afford. They possess profound and expansive artistic appeal not to be expected from works of lesser dimensions.

In the treatment of subject matter, the figures are not deployed in hand-to-hand combat or presented in ceremonial procession as is so often seen in the carvings and frescoes of the Han (206 B.C.-220 A.D.) and Tang (618-907) dynasties. Instead, they are shown as they might be found just before a decisive battle, at a moment when everybody was itching for action against the enemy. This way of treatment leaves ample room for imagination and enables the viewer to picture for himself the scenes of soul-stirring struggle which would soon reveal themselves. It conveys more than it depicts, and the figures so treated provide not only visual pleasure but stimulate deeper thoughts by guiding the mind to roam in wider realms.

As for artistic technique, the Qin figures reveal no attempt at authenticity in detail. But it is evident that care and attention have been given, through artistic exaggeration, to refinement or condensation, to bringing out the essential features.

For instance, there is no elaborate decoration on the bodies of the figures, whose clothes are only suggested in most cases just by a few simple lines. Yet the broad shoulders, the bulging bellies and the flying lower hems of some gowns, apart from giving a certain rhythm to the build of the figures, are clearly results of artistic exaggeration meant to present the Qin soldiers as warriors of stout build and unusual prowess. The lower parts of the coats, which are spread out in a slight curve, also lend a sense of stability and strength to the warriors. For variety, the garments of a number of them fly towards the back as in a breeze, and this helps to bring out the fearless sterling qualities in the warriors.

Exquisite artistry has been applied to the sculpturing of the heads, with particular attention to facial expressions.

Frowning brows and pursed lips, for instance, depict a strong will; piercing eyes under a clouded forehead indicate a rugged or ferocious quality. The quiet and shy man is portrayed through a calm countenance with downcast eyes; an amiable character is revealed through half-open lips, raised mouth corners and narrowed eyes. Mouth gaping, eyes staring and the body leaning forward — that is the man taken by surprise. Practically all eyebrows and moustaches have been exaggerated for the sake of lucid and vivid characterization. The brows that are more protruding and the moustaches more curled up than they are found by the anatomist in actual life do not strike the spectator as unreal but on the contrary give greater prominence and distinction to the personality of the characters. One can see immediately a bold and uninhibited man in the bushy whiskers, a fierce man in the thick and rising "handlebars", and an indomitable character behind the curly full whiskers. Then the "imperial" that levels off to the sides makes you feel it can only belong to a man always on the alert; the long beard floating in front of the chest gives an air of distinction to its owner...

A rough count reveals no less than 20 styles in Qin moustaches and beards, each sculpted in harmony with the expression on the face of the one it belongs to. Then there are the eyes, windows through which the inner world of the individual is revealed. They, too, received the focus of attention from the Qin sculptors. One of the unique achievements of the ancient artists is the successful portrayal of individual dispositions and temperaments through skilful shaping of moustache, beard and eyes.

Yet the Qin figures are characterized by graphic realism, having been modelled on the authentic soldiers of the Qin army with true-to-life details of dress and armour. The appearance of the figures tells with relative certainty where their living models came from. For instance, the man with the wide forehead, thick lips and broad cheeks, so simple and honest, looks like a recruit from the original state of Qin (roughly today's Shaanxi Province). The man with the round face, pointed chin and alert expression could only have come from what is present-day Sichuan. A third figure most certainly was fashioned after a native of Gansu because of the high cheekbones, large ears, thin eyelids, solid build and intrepid air.... This agrees with information from historical sources that the Qin army was composed of men mainly from the state itself or what was known as Guanzhong area (today's Shaanxi plus parts of Hubei and Sichuan provinces), mixed with recruits from other ethnic localities. The Qin figures, however, are not works of photographic accuracy; they represent images more typical than life through artistic recreation.

The decorative techniques shown by the figures are also highly varied. Noticeable examples of ornamentation include the various effects of marcelling produced by means of a comb and a rod-like tool. Decorative patterns are often found in pre-Qin bronzes, which the creators of the Qin figures inherited and used to good effect. They also employed the various techniques of sculpture — from full-relief to bas-relief carving to line cutting — and achieved a successful combination of these and all other popular skills known to folk sculptors to give body, mass, shape, expression, colour and texture to the clay they worked with. It would be safe to say that the Qin figures embody all the traditional techniques of the Chinese art of sculpture and that they doubtlessly had great influence on sculpture in later generations.

Judged anatomically, the Qin figures are not entirely accurate in proportion and shape, yet most of them show good proportion and the bone joints and muscles reasonably arranged.

To sum up, the Qin figures are fine products of a mature sculptural art developed by craftsmen who lived at the bottom rung of the social ladder but who were gifted with keen powers of observation and expression. They represent a brilliant genre of sculpture handed down from ancient China, and they mark the Qin as a new period in the development of the art, which exerted profound influence on the Han, Tang and still later dynasties. They are of epoch-making significance in the history of sculpture.

C. THE MAKING OF THE FIGURES

The making of the figures may be roughly divided into three major stages — moulding, firing and painting — each stage entailing many steps. For the sake of clarity, these will be described in the following paragraphs.

1) MOULDING

Studies reveal that the terracotta figures were moulded from carefully selected and prepared materials. The chief materials were the yellow loess and white quartz from the northern slopes of Lishan Mountain. The earth was first sifted and washed to remove the impurities so that the finished figures would appear pure, clean and even-toned in colour. The quartz was ground fine, then mixed with water and the earth in a certain ratio. the mixture was then tempered by repeated kneading and beating into a wet clay with the right degree of firmness.

Then the work proceeded from the fashioning of the roughcast, which was built from the base up, to the carving of the details. More specifically, the modelling of the figures included the following steps.

First, a square pedestal board measuring 32 × 32 cm and 3-4 cm thick was moulded. In some cases the feet of the figure were simultaneously cast in the same mould; in others they were modelled separately and then stuck on the board.

The second step was fixing the legs onto the heels. The legs were of two types: solid ones modelled from clay rolls and hollow ones modelled from clay strips.

The third step was covering the upper parts of the legs with clay strips to form the breeches. When these were somewhat dried in the shade, the lower trunk was built on top with clay.

Fourth, the same clay-strip moulding technique was employed to add the upper trunk to the lower, then when it was more or less dried, the upper chest was added. In some cases it appears that the two parts were first modelled separately and then joined together.

The fifth step was the moulding of the arms. This might be done in either of two ways — modelled separately and then luted onto the trunk or modelled directly from the chest.

The head and hands, as the sixth step, were made separately and then luted on the figure. The modelling of the head was rather complex and did not follow a uniform method. Briefly, a rough form of the head was cast in a mould; the plaited hair and bun were fashioned from extra clay spread on the roughcast; the ears and neck, made separately, were luted on; and the eyes, nose, mouth and hair strands were brought out by careful carving and incising.

The roughcast for the head was generally made in a mould of two halves, one half for the shape of the face and the other for that of the back. when both were filled with clay, the two halves were closed to produce the form of the whole head. In some cases, however, the head is found to have been cast in an oval, one-piece mould that showed the features of the face only. The rest of the head was moulded by hand. Then the two parts were stuck together, and the neck and ears fixed, to complete the general shape of the head. Ears, in all cases, were cast in one-piece moulds. Hair buns were modelled by hand or out of two-piece moulds and then luted on the head.

The roughcasts for the hands were made variously. Those with extended fingers were mostly cast in two-piece moulds. The half-clenched fist was either entirely shaped by hand or by a mixed method — the palm in moulds and the fingers by hand.

The figure was now basically shaped. What remained was carving out the details. As preparation, a thin layer of fine clay was spread over the figure. Or, the rough form was smoothed by scraping and polishing.

The carvings on the body show a rugged style of brevity in neat and simple lines. The folds of clothes, borders of collars and cuffs of the sleeves are expressed in intaglio — thick cuts for major folds and thin lines for complex pleats or wrinkles. The skilful alternation in the use of contrasting techniques — between simplicity and complexity, and between thick and fine lines — lends a richness to variety and coherence.

The armour coverings were mostly brought out by low-relief cutting into the groundwork. In a few cases, however, additional clay seems to have been spread on for carving out the armour. The studs and straps of the armour were pressed on with moulds. Straight lines were employed for the carving of the hard plates, while flowing lines were used to bring out the soft and light texture of the clothing.

The head, hand, foot and leg attest to the painstaking meticulousness with which they were carved. The braided hair stands out in low-relief — an effect achieved by intaglio lines cut into the ground or into extra, spread-on clay. The hair bun was given a convincing appearance by a combination of techniques — full-relief and bas-relief carving plus incision. Strands of hair were set out by a variety of ways — pressed out with a comb-like tool in straight and curving lines, rolled with a rod-like tool into spirals of hair locks (as often seen on the heads of Buddha portraits of the Sui and Tang periods), or hand-modelled into undulations and then incised in intaglio. Of these three methods in sculpting the hair style, the first two are highly decorative, while the last brings out fully the texture of the hair.

The focus of emphasis in carving was placed on the facial features. Some eyebrows, modelled in high-relief, were made to protrude like hills to show a dogged and intrepid character; others were so finely done that lines in intaglio were cut to give the effect of separate eyebrow hairs.

All eyes were clearly and correctly modelled, with the upper eyelids folding over the lower lids at the corners, and with the inside corner of the eye lower than the outside one. But they run the gamut of human expressions from glowering in anger to being narrowed in a smile. Eyes, as windows on the soul, on the Qin figures are certainly well done and rich in expression.

Also given due share of attention were the wrinkles on the older faces and the rounded fullness of the young ones. And one can see a conscious effort to achieve harmony between the facial muscles and the feelings of the individual.

The moustaches and beards are as varied in form as the methods employed in delineating them. Some were carved from extra clay spread on, others were made separately and then luted on, and still others were given shape and form by cutting into the groundwork. As a rule, the general shapes of the beards were made first, with the details added later by means of incised lines.

In short, meticulous work was done on the face to produce a vividness that distinguishes one figure from another in mood and disposition.

The carving of the hand agrees with what is known in modern anatomy in the length and thickness of the fingers and in the varying shapes of the muscles with the stretching and bending of the joints. The legs and feet were so scraped, polished and carved that the hardness of the bones and the firmness of the flesh are manifest. Other details, like the way the foot is shaped (more arched on the side of the big toe than on the other side), the roundness of the standing leg and the flatness of the bending and taut leg, were all well depicted after life.

The modelling of the pottery horse went through the same process: first the roughcast and then detailed carving. The roughcast was made in two steps.

The first step was the making of the separate parts of the horse — head, neck, body, leg, ear and tail. The head was cast in a mould consisting of two equal halves, the left and the right half. The muzzle was modelled by hand and luted on. The legs, being hard and solid like stone, must have been made of clay which had been repeatedly beaten and tempered. The neck and trunk were formed of pre-made clay parts: the neck generally of two halves left and right, and the trunk of three sections (the hindquarters, belly and chest, which were in turn made of there or four pieces of clay). The ear and tail were modelled by hand.

The second step was assembling the pre-fabricated parts. It began with the legs, which were erected at fixed points to carry the weight they were to carry. This was done with the assistance of other props to prevent the legs from becoming deformed under pressure. Then the trunk was laid on the legs and auxiliary props, first the clay pieces for the belly, then those for the sides and finally the back, in the same order as the building of a house — first the foundation, then the walls and finally the roof.

The different parts were joined together by means of lute, which was smeared at the joints and on their outside and inside surfaces to strengthen them. The assembled horse was then beaten to make the joining tight and firm.

To prevent the trunk from going out of shape, a framework of wooden boards was arranged inside to hold it in place. After the rough shape of the trunk was completed, the pre-made neck, head and tail were fixed on in that order. Every joining was plastered over with lute and repeatedly beaten for firmness. To prevent the neck and head from falling off in the process, they were propped up with a T-shaped support until they were securely luted.

Now the horse was roughly in shape. It was then smeared over with a thin coating of fine clay, and the carving of the details began.

The legs were scraped and carved to bring out their vigour and strength. The hindquarters were made smooth by polishing and beating to show the well-muscled fleshiness of the animal. Extra clay was thrown on the chest to form bulging chest muscles.

For the head of the horse, curved lines in intaglio were employed to carve out the eyelids, nostrils and corners of the mouth. The eyeballs were made noticeable and life-like by deep cuts around them.

Viewed as a whole, the horse is modelled with exactitude and in good proportion. The trunk, presented with neat simplicity, is free from over-elaboration. The limbs, comprising many straight lines cut with bold strokes, show a rugged style and skilled craftsmanship. The head looks vigorously lean and bony under the skin. All of this indicates that the terracotta horses, gems like the human figures, were sculpted by the hands of talented masters of olden times.

Technically speaking, for the sculpture of the Qin figures, the six methods (moulding, throwing-on, finger-modelling, luting, carving and painting) known to the traditional folk artist were all employed to perfection to bring out the effects of body, mass, shape, expression, colour and texture.

For large, full-relief figures, a roughcast was first made by means of moulds or hand-modelling to give the object its body, mass and shape. On this base, surface decoration was added in bas-relief by throwing on clay, finger-modelling and luting. The details were then added by means of carved or incised lines to show the expression and indisposition of the object. Thanks to this masterly execution, the finished objects are marked by a richness in depth and by distinctive individual characters.

It is amazing that as early as two millenia ago people had already mastered the various methods of sculpture and developed a whole set of techniques characteristically Chinese. The Qin tomb figures stand to testify to the dexterity and wisdom of the working people of the Qin Dynasty who carried the art of sculpture to such great heights.

2) FIRING AND PAINTING

The clay figures, after being modelled and dried in the shade, were placed in the kiln for firing. The structure of the kilns is still unknown, as none of them have been excavated. However, we know that most brick kilns of the Qin Dynasty were built partially underground, and consisted of a baking chamber, a fire chamber, a stove door and other parts. The baking chamber might be square, oblong or horseshoe in shape. The square type was larger than the other two, and measured about five square metres in space. As the pottery warriors and horses are works of full scale, they were presumably fired in square kiln chambers.

The key to successful pottery baking lies in correctly regulating the temperature of the fire. *Tian Gong Kai Wu* (1637), the famous Ming Dynasty encyclopaedia on ancient crafts and trades has this to say about brick baking:

> When the fire is slightly under the correct temperature, the colour of the baked brick will be rusty and dull; when the fire is much under, the brick will be motley-coloured and, when weathered in frost or snow, will crumble and be reduced to earth again.

> When the fire is slightly over the correct temperature, the brick will crack on the surface; when the fire is much over, the brick will be useless, for it will shrink, break or twist and sound like scrap iron when struck.

Unlike this description, all the Qin tomb figures unearthed show even firing, a pure bluish grey colour, great hardness, no parts broken, cracked or deformed by under-baking or over-firing. In other words all signs indicate that they were fired to perfection. Tests have determined that the kiln temperatue used for the Qin figures was high, between 900 and 1,000 degrees Centigrade.

A clay figure so large in size must shrink at a certain rate when it is dried in the shade and when fired in the kiln, and is liable to go out of shape unless correctly handled. The potters who made the Qin figures proved their worth by successfully tackling the problem of shrinkage. This shows that a rich store of experience had already been accumulated from a long period of productive practice by the time of the Qin, including a high level of skill in kiln temperature control.

Another problem that had to be tackled is the varying thickness of different parts of the clay figure — from 2-3 cm for the walls of the body cavity of the human figure to more than 10 cm at the legs or the hems of the clothing, from 2-4 cm for the walls of the horse body to 10-15 cm at the hind quarters. This uneven thickness could cause uneven firing, leaving the thick parts under-baked and the thin parts over-burnt. To solve this problem, the Qin potters and kilnmen devised a number of clever methods. They made many flues in the kiln and, on the thick parts of the figure they drilled holes or cut grooves, or made them hollow — all this to ensure the even distribution of firing.

After being baked in the kiln, the human and horse figures acquired an all-over bluish grey colour. They were then painted to show the different colour patterns of clothing and harness. But as we see them now, the overwhelming majority have been burnt in wars and eroded by ground water over a period of more than two millenia so they have lost their original paint except for a few traces of bright colour here and there. The range of colours found so far on the figures include vermilion, claret, pink, green, light green, light purple, blue, azure, yellow, orange, black, white and ochre, all of mineral source. The process of painting involved a preliminary coating of glue to fasten the colours which were applied over it.

A few of the pottery pieces yielded by Vault 2 have rather well preserved colours, making it possible to visualize how the figures must have looked in their day.

The figure for a general for example, excavated from Block 4 of Vault 2 is clad in a vermilion undergown covered by a dark purple coat with vermilion lace at the cuffs and collar. Over that, he wears a coloured breastplate of armour composed of ochre-coloured, fine "fish-scale" plates and decked with vermilion studs and straps. Colourful patterns adorn the borders of the armour, the collar, the chest and the back. the équalières of the armour, too, are fringed with patterned borders around a yellow ground painted over with two or three flowers. Bright ribbons are knotted, with their loose ends fluttering, under the chin, on the chest, at the back and shoulders. The legs of the general are in bluish-green trousers, which reach down to a pair of ochre shoes with raised toes. For headgear he has a dark-purple "pheasant cap" tied with orange ribbons. His hands are held before the abdomen as if poised on the hilt of sword. Chin up and chest out, he looks the picture of imposing nobility.

Unearthed together with the general was the figure of an officer somewhat junior in rank. He is clad in a long green coat with vermilion borders at the collar and cuffs. His suit of armour, covering the chest and shoulders, is composed of ochre-coloured plates, vermilion studs and straps, and edged in white. Coloured geometric patterns adorn the collar and the straps at the back. The rest of his array includes claret trousers, dark ochre shoes with raised toes and an officer's cap of the same colour. His face and hands are painted pink, and the eyebrows and moustache black. The eyes, coloured in black and white, appear bright.

Also worth noting is a kneeling figure out of Block 10 of Vault 2. He is clad in a long green coat with vermilion borders at the collar and cuffs. His ochre-coloured armour has vermilion studs and straps. He wears dark-blue trousers,

purplish puttees, and ochre shoes adorned with purplish borders. His hair is worn in a round bun fastened with vermilion ribbons on top of his head.

The colouring of the pottery horses, in comparison, is relatively simple. On the whole, claret is evenly applied except on the mane and tail, which are painted black, and the hoofs, which are white.

The colours applied on the figures, generally speaking, appear to be lucid, lively and bright. Used on the upper garments, they range from vermilion, claret, dark and light green, dark and light purple, to light blue or azure. As a rule, a vermilion coat was matched with green or blue trousers; green or blue coats went with reddish trousers. The matching of contrasting colours seems to help set off the awe-inspiring atmosphere of the battle array of a magnificent army. In a word, one finds in the Qin figures a happy integration of sculpture and painting, which combine to enhance the artistic effects of the finished works.

VI. MAKERS OF THE QIN FIGURES

Who were the creators of the terracotta army? How many workers turned out the eight thousand warriors and horses? This is a question of keen interest, but without a definite answer.

In the course of excavating and restoring the figures over many years, the author has found a number of names engraved or seal-marked on some pottery warriors and horses in almost hidden places. These are the names or seal-marks of the creators of the terracotta army. These potters living at the bottom of the social scale of the Qin Empire had come either from imperial potteries which catered for the court or from private popular workshops.

Eighty names have been found, all of masters in the art. Each must have had a number of assistants of apprentices working under them. Calculated on the basis of some dozen helpers per master, the eight thousand terracotta figures would have been produced by about a thousand men, quite an impressive army of artists themselves. It is mind-boggling that so many artists should have remained "buried" for more than two thousand years. Their re-emergence can only be hailed as a major event in the art and culture of Chinese and world history.

A. THE POTTER-SCULPTORS

The Chinese characters, engraved or impressed on some of the figures tell the names of the potter-sculptors. There are also serial numbers. The names may be divided into four groups:

1) Those preceded by the Chinese character "宫" (gong), hereinafter called "gong names" for convenience;

2) Names preceded by the Chinese character "右" (you) or "大" (da), which we shall call "you names" or "da names" reseptively;

3) Personal names preceded by place names, and

4) Names without other qualifiers.

The first two groups refer to master-potters who came from potteries operated by central government authorities. Group 3 represent those who came from local workshops. Group 4, being merely personal names, offer no clue as to where the potters came from.

1) POTTERS BEARING GONG NAMES

Most of these *gong* names were impressed on the figures by means of seals; a few were engraved. There are altogether 10 names beginning with the character *gong* "宫", for instance Gong Jiang, Gong De, Gong Xi and Gong Zang.

It is known that under the Qin, there was a government department by the name of Gong Shui "宫水", whose principal duty was to make bricks and tiles for palace and mausoleum projects. Many of the *gong* names like Gong Jiang, Gong De, Gong Xi and Gong Zang have also been found on the bricks and tiles discovered on the grounds of the Emperor's Mausoleum.

That the same names should appear on both the figures and the tiles cannot be a mere coincidence. The vaults with the terracotta army are a part of Qin Shi Huang's necropolis; the making of the figures for the pottery army and that of the bricks and tiles for the mausoleum could not have been far apart in time, so it is assumed that the names which appeared on both types of products belonged to the same persons. That means the potters who made the figures were the same craftsmen who made the bricks and tiles. They must have been experienced potters under central court administration specially selected for making the terracotta figures.

2) POTTERS BEARING *DA* AND *YOU* NAMES

The names found on three figures — two unearthed from Vault 1 and one from Vault 2 — begin with the character *da* "大". The same names have been found on bricks and tiles unearthed in the area of the Emperor's necropolis. One of the three is "大匠" (*Da Jiang*), an abbreviation for "将作大匠" (*Jiang Zuo Da Jiang*). The latter was a central government department under the Western Han Dynasty (206 B.C. - A.D. 24), which immediately followed the Qin, and presumably already existed during the Qin. It was in charge of constructing palace buildings and other royal engineering projects and the making of bricks and tiles. There is reason to believe a name bearing the character *da* "大" or *jiang* "匠" refers to that department and the character following it represents the personal name of the craftsman. If this conjecture is correct, it means that some of the workmen of the potteries under the central department "Jiang Zuo Da Jiang" were also selected and transferred to the job of making the terracotta army.

The character "右" (*you*) has been found inscribed on two figures from Vault 1. One has the character standing alone and the other has it in combination, namely "右亥" (*You Hai*). The character *You* was a shortened form of *You Si Kong* "右司空", a department under one of the ministries of public works, while the word *Hai* was the name of the potter. Many bricks and tiles bearing the character *you* have been found among the ruins of Xianyang, capital of the Qin Dynasty, and of Emperor Qin Shi Huang's mausoleum. That tells us potters in the workshops under *You Si Kong*, or a *you* department responsible for the production of bricks and tiles, were also conscripted for the making of the terracotta army.

3) POTTERS FROM VARIOUS LOCALITIES

On some of the figures a total of 21 names have been found to be preceded by place names — Xianyang, Liyang, Linjin and Anyi. Xianyang is the most common, as in the names Xianyang Chu, Xianyang Xing, Xianyang Jing, Xianyang Lu and others. In some cases Xianyang is abbreviated as *Xian*, as in Xian Chu, Xian Xing, and Xian Jing.

The place names before personal names naturally indicated where the persons came from. And the most frequent recurrence of Xianyang should be no surprise as Xianyang was the political, economic and cultural centre of the country with a well-developed pottery industry and many experienced potters. It would only be natural that potters of Xianyang were called up for the important project of making the terracotta army.

Up to the time of writing, only about one fifth of the total area of the vaults has been excavated. More potters' names are expected to be brought to light as the excavation continues over the entire ground. It is probable that other place names will appear, telling that potters from places other than Xianyang, Liyang, Linjin and Anyi also took part in making the pottery figures.

4) OTHER POTTERS

Grouped under this title are potters' names with no qualifiers as to place or department to indicate where they came from. These names generally comprise only one Chinese character; a few have two. So far forty-six of this type have been found, including Yongliu, Xiaosu, Qu, Wen, Tian, Wang, Wu, and Zhong.

Altogether eighty names of the above four descriptions have been counted. Why, then, were potters' names inscribed on the warrior and horse figures? This was evidently meant to enforce control over the quantity and quality produced. According to *Lü's Spring and Autumn,* an ancient work completed just before the state of Qin united all China, "The finished product is inscribed with the craftsman's name so that his performance may be checked. If he falls short of the requirement he will be penalized accordingly, and investigation will be made into the cause."

The incription of the potters' names on their works was primarily a means by which the authorities of the Qin court exercised strict control and supervision over the potters, yet by this measure they unwittingly helped to preserve for posterity the names of many ancient sculptor-artists. These names, together with the jewel of the Qin figure art itself, will go down in history for ever.

B. DIFFERENCES IN STYLE

Of the four groups of potters enumerated in the foregoing paragraphs, the first and second groups came from workshops under central government departments, and the third group came from local potteries. While it is difficult to tell the origins of the potters listed in the fourth group, it may be said, judging by their styles, that most were from the localities and a small number were from official workshops. In short, the potter-sculptors may be broadly divided into two categories: those from workshops under central authorities and those from local areas. Obvious differences in style can be detected between the two categories in the works they produced.

In point of bodily form, the terracotta figures made by the potters from central department workshops are of strong and hefty build, and make stalwart images of firm and unshakable strength. The qualities their makers sought to express seem to have been resoluteness and bravery.

On the other hand, the figures made by the sculptors from local potteries are mostly delicate in physical form expressed in flowing lines. Some have broad shoulders and wasp waists, the lower hems of their gowns curved like bells. Others are tall but slender, characterized by an air of distinction. Still others look small and thin, and devoid of physical strength. All this constitutes in one way or another a sharp contrast with the vigorous and robust style one sees in the terracotta warriors sculptured by the potters from central government workshops.

In the modelling of faces and facial expressions, the potter-sculptors from central department workshops generally produced square, rectangular or round faces with bushy eyebrows, large eyes, broad mouths, thick lips, ample foreheads and high cheekbones — features typical of Qin people of the Guanzhong area. And the qualities seen behind such faces are simplicity, rustic honesty, solemnity and physical vigour — qualities characteristic of the palace guards.

The faces of the warrior figures made by potters from local areas varied widely in shape: round, square, oblong, elongated, narrow, broad of forehead but pointed of chin, and so on. Some may look plump and sturdy, others quite thin, and still others very long. The dispositions presented by them are as varied as life, and carry with them an authentic appeal of familiarity and freshness.

In artistry, the potters from workshops under central authorities generally show a high level of skill in carving and modelling. The warriors made by them are well-proportioned and accurately shaped, generally in keeping with the principles of human anatomy. They also show rich experience in kiln work in that the figures are mostly bluish grey in colour and hard in texture — signs of even, well-regulated firing.

The local potters exhibit an unevenness in the skills at their command: some consummate but others quite inferior. Although many of their works are excellent, some are definitely puerile and lack proportion.

The differences in skill and style between the two categories of potters are due to differences in their living circumstances and life experiences, and in their abilities of expression. Such differences will naturally lead to the creation of different artistic images. This is particularly true in the feudal society in which handicrafts were handed down from master to apprentice, from father to son. Confined within the family or guild system, they tended to be conservative and tied to narrow traditions of training. With the same subject or theme, artists from different environments or different sects of schooling would produce art images far apart in style.

The potters belonging to central government departments had constant contact with the royal guards and, through what they saw and heard, were quite familiar with their looks and ways. And the warriors on guard duty at the imperial palaces had been carefully selected and were the elite among the military units, strong of build, valiant and brave in spirit. They became the natural models after whom the potter-sculptors created the images of Qin soldiers. Therefore, the terracotta warriors done by them look like the palace guards, towering and awe-inspiring.

Furthermore, these potters lived and worked together in the imperial potteries: in craftsmanship they tended to influence and learn from each other. Naturally they formed a common modelling style and artistic technique. Meanwhile, the strict discipline enforced by the officials in charge of handicraft administration also contributed to their meticulous and painstaking work style.

The potters from local potteries, on the other hand, had lived among the broad masses of the people. They were familiar with all types of people with different builds, different faces and different dispositions. It was only natural that they took the people around them as models for the sculpturing of the terracotta warriors. The realm from which they drew their material proved to be much wider, more representative of

society at large. The pottery figures produced by them, therefore, are more varied and colourful.

At the same time, these local potters had been influenced by different masters, and they were unequal in mastery of sculpturing skills. Hence a marked lack of uniformity in art level in the works they created.

The makers of the terracotta army at Emperor Qin Shi Huang's mausoleum — gems of ancient Chinese sculpture — were the potter-sculptors called up from official and private potteries. They were the real creators of the Qin figures. But they must have worked according to certain designs or "blueprints." Who were the designers of the blueprints?

No record can be found in ancient literature to answer this question. But it was Li Si, the Prime Minister, who was in overall charge of the project of the Emperor's mausoleum. It is highly likely that Li and other ministers had a hand in the designing of the terracotta army vaults, which were an important part of the Emperor's necropolis. The design of the vaults, of course, must also have had the sanction of Qin Shi Huang himself so that his wishes and demands were met.

In paying tribute to the potter-sculptors for their brilliant achievements, sight must not be lost of the parts played by the designers and supervisors of the grand project. It was they who worked out the general layout and laid down the general theme of the terracotta army; it was also they who organized and administered the making of the figures.

But this organization and administration was compulsory in nature, even to the point of ruthlessness. And that accounts for one of the major differences between the Qin figure art and Western sculpture. Western artists could express their own ideas to a large extent in their art creations. The creators of the Qin figures, however, worked under rigid orders and, if they had any ideas of their own to express, could only do so by veiled hints and suggestions. On the whole, the art as represented by the Qin figures embodied the ideas of the rulers, and served the interests of the new-emerging landlord class.

VII. THE WEAPONS UNEARTHED AND HOW THEY WERE MADE

The vaults containing the pottery army are also a vast armoury, out of which more than 30,000 metal weapons have been unearthed so far. Except for a very few pieces made of iron, the arms are of bronze. They include swords, spears, lances, halberds, dagger-axes, *shu, pi,* crossbow triggers, arrowheads and *wandao.* Most of these are commonly seen, but the *wandao, shu* and *pi* are rare varieties.

The *wandao* or 'curved sword' is a sabre- or scimitar-like weapon, 65.2 cm long in total length, shaped like the crescent moon, while its cross-section looks like the stone of a jujube. It has blades on both edges but its tip is flat and dull. Obviously cast with a two-piece split mould, it was finished by grinding and sharpening. This weapon had never been seen before. The absence of a sharp point coupled with the presence of blades on both edges of the new moon shape indicate that it was a weapon not meant for stabbing but for cutting either with the outside edge or with the inside one by pulling it back like a big hook. It is recorded in *Chronicles of Wu and Yue* that King Helu of Wu (?-496 B.C.) "ordered the making of *jingou* (literally, gold hooks)." So the orginal name for this curved sword should be *jingou,* or *wugou* (Wu hook) as it was popularly called by later writers. In fact, during a long historical epoch, from the Northern and

Southern Dynasties down to the Sui and Tang periods (roughly 5th to 10 century A.D.) it was the fashion for youths of eminent families to wear *wugou* on their belts as a symbol of bravery and status, a practice often refered to in poems of the time. For instance, "Golden halter adorns a fine horse,/ Silk belt hung with a *wugou*." (By Bao Zhao of the Southern Dynasties.) Again, "Why not wear the *wugou*/ And be man enough to recapture the fifty counties of lost land?" (by Li He of the Tang Dynasty).

The weapon *pi* had been known only by name from books, and its discovery from the Qin vaults marked the first time the actual object was seen. It looks exactly like a dagger of 30-odd centimetres long with a flat stem at the end by means of which it is fixed on a 3-metre-long wooden shaft, apparently a long, stabbing weapon rather like a spear. An account in Zuo Qiuming's *Commentaries on the Spring and Autumn Annals* has this passage: "Assassins were dispatched to murder Governor Hua Wu. There were six of them, and they did it with *pi* at the gate." It can be seen that the weapon was already in use during the Spring and Autumn Period (770-467 B.C.). However, when the *pi* is seen without its wooden shaft, it may be easily mistaken for a dagger. This may be the reason why it was never reported among archaeological finds.

More than thirty weapons by the name of *shu* have been yielded by Vault 3. The *shu* is cylindrical in shape, 10.5 cm long and 2.3 cm across, with a polyhedrical pointed head. When unearthed, they were found bundled together with what remained, about one metre long, of their wooden shafts.

Explaining this weapon, *Shi Ming*, an early 3rd-century etymological dictionary has this entry: "*Shu*, ... 12 *chi* long (about 3-4 metres), has no blade." A striking weapon, it could not hook, stab or cut, so it would be moe suitable for purposes of self-defence than otherwise. Initially one of the five weapons (spear, lance, *shu*, dagger-axe and bow) wielded by the chariot-borne warrior, it became more and more a ceremonial weapon, mostly held by palace guards. Han Fei (c. 280-233 B.C.), for instance, has the following story to tell in his principal work:

> The law of Chu forbade the crown prince to ride in a carriage up to the gate of the palace. Once in a heavy rain the king ordered an urgent audience with the prince. As there were puddles of water in the courtyard, the prince rode right up to the gate of the royal residence. The lictors raised their *shu* at the horses, crushing the carriage.

Among the weapons unearthed from Vault 3, the *shu* predominates in number, providing further proof that the warrior figures in it represented members of an important bodyguard.

The weapons excavated from the Qin tomb vaults are not only noted for their immense numbers but also for the advanced techniques with which they were made. The bronze weapons, cast in two-piece split moulds, were well filed, ground and burnished into the finished products. They have regular and well-defined edges, sharp blades and points, a smooth surface finish and a hardness corresponding to that of medium carbon steel after treatment. Tests have shown that the alloying elements of various weapons are as follows:

Bronze swords:
    copper   71 - 74.6%
    tin   21.38 - 31%
    lead   1.14 - 2.18%
    with traces of 12 other rare metals
Bronze arrowheads:
    copper   80.11 - 83.06%
    tin   11.1 - 12.5%
    zinc   0.13%

Bronze lances:
    copper   69.62%
    tin   30.38%
Bronze *chun* (a kind of drum):
    copper   84.83%
    tin   15.15%

According to *Kao Gong Ji*, an authoritative work on various crafts written in the 5th century B.C.:

> There are six specifications for the preparation of copper alloys. With one-sixth being tin, it is the alloy for bells and tripods; with one-fifth being tin, it is the alloy for battle-axes; with one quarter being tin, it is the alloy for lances and halberds; with one-third being tin, it is the alloy for broadswords; with two-fifths being tin, it is the alloy for arrowheads; with half being tin, it is the alloy for bronze mirrors and flints.

The tin content in the alloy, it can be seen, decides the texture and hardness of the objects made of it. Of the weapons from the Qin vaults, the ratio between copper and tin is approximately as follows:

    swords   3 : 1⁻
    lances   2.3 : 1⁻
    arrowheads   7 : 1⁺
    bronze drums 5.6 : 1⁻

Compared with the specifications given in *Kao Gong Ji*, the composition of the Qin swords and lances approaches that of "the alloys for broadswords," but that of the arrowheads is very much at variance with the directions of the earlier book. The Qin arrowheads, however, show a sizable content of lead, which should also increase the hardness of the metal. This shows that the Qin people were well-versed in the art of weaponry, able to vary the formulae for arms to suit different purposes. It has been demonstrated in practice that bronze with a 17-20% tin content is the toughest and most resilient, and bronze with a 30-40% tin content is the hardest but most brittle. The weapons found in the Qin tomb vaults are of the right hardness, being made according to appropriate specifications.

What is particularly worthy of attention is that the swords and arrowheads are found by electronic probing and fluoroscopic analysis to have a compact oxide coating, about 10-15 microns thick, containing a compound of chromium. Thanks to this anticorrosive and rust-resistant coating, the weapons, especially the bronze swords, still have glistening surfaces although they have been buried undergound for over two thousand years.

The technology of chrome-plating was developed in Europe and America only in modern times, yet it was already mastered as early as the Qin in China. And the discovery of compounds of chromium is not an isolated case at the Qin Mausoleum. An oxide of chromium has also been found on the bronze arrowheads excavated from the tomb of Liu Sheng or Prince Jing of Zhongshan (?-113 B.C.) of early Han Dynasty. This strengthens the belief that the advanced technique of chrome-plating was well-known to Chinese more than two millenia ago — a miracle in the history of metallurgy and a great contribution made by China to science and technology in the ancient world.

Note: This article is based on other of my published writings and contains information and passages from them, namely: *The First Emperor's Terracotta Legion* by China Travel and Tourism Press, and Wenwu Publishing House, both in 1983, the *Makers of the Qin Tomb Figures* carried in the periodical *Wenbo*, No.4, 1986

The Author

PLATES
CATALOGUE

1、將軍俑 (一號俑坑出土)
2、一號兵馬俑坑全景

1. A terra-cotta general unearthed from
   No.1
2. A panoramic view of Pit No.1

3. 將軍俑：他雙手交垂于腹前，作拄劍狀
（一號俑坑出土）。

3. A terra-cotta general with his hands crossed over his abdomen in the gesture of leaning on a sword, unearthed from Pit No.1

4、軍吏俑(二號俑坑出土)。

4. A terra-cotta officer unearthed from Pit No.2

5、中級軍吏俑: 他身穿前後下襬平齊的甲
衣, 雙肩有長大的披膊(即肩甲), 頭戴長
冠(一號俑坑出土)。

5. A terra-cotta officer of middle rank was
unearthed from Pit No.1. He wears evenly-
rimmed armour and a long cap with long
gauntlets over his shoulders.

6、下級軍吏俑

6. A terra-cotta officer of low rank.

7、鎧甲俑(一號俑坑出土)

7 A terra-cotta armoured warrior unearthed from Pit No.1

8、立射俑(二號俑坑出土)

8. A terra-cotta archer at a standing position unearthed from Pit No.2

9. 袍俑：他身穿長襦，腰束革帶，腿紮行
縢(即裹腿)，足穿方口齊頭履，頭綰圓
髻，右手作提弓狀(一號俑坑出土)。

9. A battle-robed warrior unearthed from Pit
No.1 wears a long garment which is tied by a
leather belt at his waist. With his legs lashed
with wrappings, he wears square-opening,
up-turned shoes. His hair is tied in a bun, and
his right hand seems to hold a bow.

10、車士俑

10. A terra-cotta chariot soldier

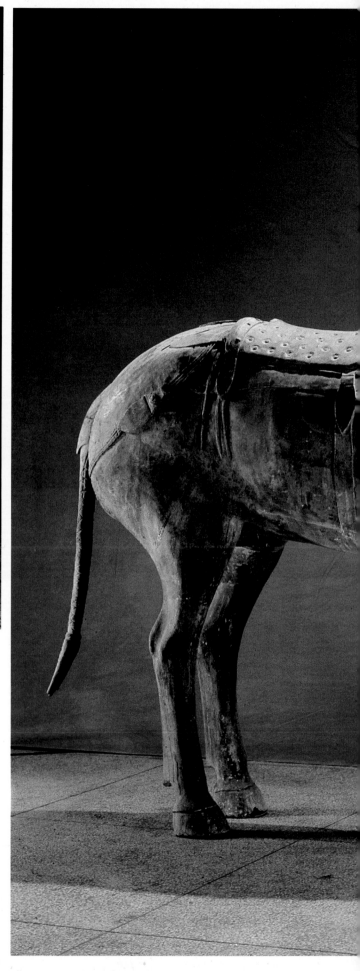

11、御手俑(一號俑坑出土)
12、騎兵俑:他身穿胡服,外披短甲,足登短
　　靴,體型修長,英姿勃勃(二號俑坑出
　　土)。

11. A terra-cotta charioteer unearthed from Pit No.1
12. A terra-cotta cavalryman unearthed from Pit No.2 wears the Hu's costume and a pair of boots. He has short armour draped over his shoulders, looking slim, bright and brave.

13、秦始皇陵遠景

14、秦始皇陵

13. Mausoleum of Emperor Qin Shi Huang at a distance

14. Mausoleum of Emperor Qin Shi Huang

15、發掘現場的一角
16、發掘現場的一角(一號俑坑)
17、一號兵馬俑坑東端出土的陶俑和建築
　　遺迹

15. A view of an excavation site
16. A view of an excavation site of Pit No.1
17. Terra-cotta figures and remains of construction unearthed from the eastern end of Pit No.1

18、 俑坑的建築遺迹：坑底用青色條磚墁
    鋪，隔牆的兩側每隔1.4米有一根木
    柱，木柱因經火焚僅存炭迹。
19、 一號兵馬俑坑南邊門的便道
20、 一號兵馬俑坑東南角的磚牆，是保存下
    來的我國最早的一段磚牆。
21、 棚木炭迹(一號俑坑)
22、 棚木遺迹(一號俑坑)

18. The remains of construction of a pit: the pit
    floor is paved with blue bricks; there was
    one wooden post at every 1.4m. along
    either side of every partition wall. Now
    only the carbonized posts are visible
    because of the fire.
19. A side passage at the southern entrance of
    Pit No.1
20. The brick wall in the southeast corner of Pit
    No.1 is the earliest wall preserved in China
    so far.
21. Carbonized rafters of Pit No.1
22. Remains of rafters of Pit No.1

23、蓆紋印痕(一號俑坑)

24、一號兵馬俑坑東端陶俑的出土情況

25、陶俑出土情況(一號俑坑)

23. Impressions of mat patterns of Pit No.1

24. Excavation of terra-cotta figures at the eastern end of Pit No.1

25. Terra-cotta warriors under excavation in Pit No.1

26、陶馬出土現狀(一號俑坑)
27、發掘現場的一角(一號俑坑)
28、陶俑、陶馬出土情況(一號俑坑)
29、陶俑身上的印文"宮彊"(印文爲陶俑作者的名字,一號俑坑)。

26. Terra-cotta horses under excavation in Pit No.1
27. A view of excavation site of Pit No.1
28. Excavation of terra-cotta warriors and horses of Pit No.1
29. " 宮 ", an inscription of pottery-figure maker's name born on a terra-cotta warrior's body of Pit No.1

30、木製馬車輪的遺迹(一號俑坑)

31、陶俑出土情況(一號俑坑)

32、考古工作者在精心地清除陶俑頭部的
　　泥土(一號俑坑)

30. Remains of a wooden wheel of a chariot in
Pit No.1

31. Excavation of terra-cotta figures of Pit
No.1

32. The archaeologists meticulously dressing a
terra-cotta warrior's head in Pit No.1

33、陶俑出土現狀(一號俑坑)
34、銅戟出土現狀(一號俑坑)
35、騎兵俑出土情况(二號俑坑)

33. Terra-cotta warriors in Pit No.1 under excavation
34. A bronze halberd being excavated from Pit No.1
35. Excavation of cavalrymen of Pit No.2

36、三號坑內景
37、考古人員發掘三號坑
38、秦俑發現人和最早發掘人，左起：楊志
　　發、袁仲一、楊天義、程學華、楊鵬躍。

36. An interior view of Pit No.3
37. Archaeologists excavating Pit No.3
38. The discoverers and the first excavators of
　　the terra-cotta army of the Qin dynasty:
　　Yang Zhifa, Yuan Zhongyi, Yang Tianyi,
　　Cheng Xuehua and Yang Pengyao (from
　　left to right).

39、一號銅車馬

39. No.1 bronze chariot and horses

40、二號銅車馬　　　　　　　　　40. No.2 bronze chariot and horses

41、銅車馬發掘坑
42、銅車馬的發掘

41. The excavation pit of the bronze chariots and horses
42. The excavation of the bronze chariots and horses

43、秦始皇兵馬俑博物館外景(一號俑坑大廳)

43. The exterior view of the hall housing Pit No.1 of Emperor Qin Shi Huang's Terracotta Army Museum

44、一號兵馬俑坑，軍陣前列隊形。　　　44. Front ranks of the battle formation of Pit
No.1

45、一號兵馬俑坑, 軍陣前列隊形(背視)。　　45. Back view of front ranks of the battle
　　　　　　　　　　　　　　　　　　　　　　formation of Pit No.1

46、 一號兵馬俑坑, 軍陣的前鋒(由北向
    南)。
47、 一號兵馬俑坑, 軍陣的前鋒部隊。

46. The vanguard of the battle formation of Pit
    No.1 (from north to south)
47. The vanguard of the battle formation of Pit
    No.1

48、一號兵馬俑坑，軍陣的一角。 48. A view of the battle formation of Pit No.1

49、步兵的隊列(一號俑坑)

50、戰車後隸屬步兵俑的队列

49. Rows of infantrymen unearthed from Pit No. 1

50. Rows of infantrymen attached to war chariots

51、戰車前後的隸屬步兵俑(一號俑坑)
52、駟馬戰車一組,及車前、車後步兵俑的
　　隊列。

51. Terra-cotta infantrymen attached to war
chariots in Pit No.1
52. A war chariot with a team of four horses
together with rows of tera-cotta
infantrymen in front of and behind chariot.

53、車迹(一號俑坑)

53. Remains of a chariot unearthed from Pit No.1

54、車馬一組(一號俑坑)
55、俑坑土隔梁的棚木槽(一號俑坑)

54. A team of a chariot and horses
55. Rafter grooves of partition walls in No.1 terra-cotta army pit

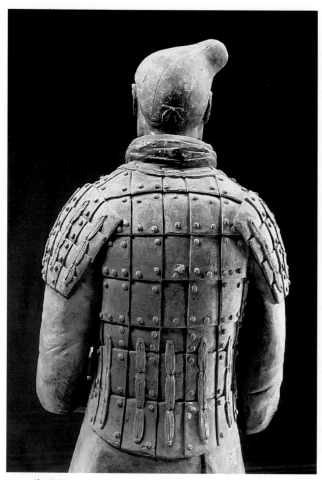 

56、將軍俑
57、鎧甲俑[背視](一號俑坑)
58、御手俑

56. A terra-cotta general
57. Terra-cotta armoured warrior unearthed
    from Pit No.1 (back view)
58. A terra-cotta charioteer

59、蹲跪俑：他左腿蹲曲，右膝着地，雙手在
　　胸的右側一上一下作控弓狀。弓竪立，
　　弓背在前，弓弦在後(二號俑坑)。

60、軍吏俑：他身穿鎧甲，頭戴長冠，左手作
　　持戈、矛等兵器狀；左手作按劍狀，面容
　　嚴肅，英姿勃勃(一號俑坑)。

61、鎧甲俑：身穿鎧甲，頭戴介幘，巍然挺
　　立，神情機敏(一號俑坑出土)。

59. A terra-cotta kneeling archer: He flexes his
    left leg and right knee on the ground. His
    hands, one above the other, are in a
    gesture of holding a bow, which seems to be
    upright with its frame in front and its string
    behind, from Pit No.2.

60. A terra-cotta officer: He is clad in armour,
    wearing a long cap, with his right hand in a
    gesture of holding a dagger-like weapon
    and left hand in a gesture of holding a
    sword, looking solemn, valiant and heroic.

61. A terra-cotta armoured warrior: He wears
    a headdress, stands imposingly, presents
    his alertness, from Pit No.1

62、鎧甲俑(一號俑坑出土)

63、車士俑頭像(二號俑坑出土)

62. A terra-cotta armoured warrior from Pit
    No.1

63. Head of a chariot soldier unearthed from
    Pit No.2

64、車士俑[正視](二號俑坑出土)

65、車士俑[背視](二號俑坑出土)

66、車士俑的手勢。手作持長兵器狀(二號
　　俑坑出土)。

67、車士俑的雙足立姿(二號俑坑出土)

64. Front view of a terra-cotta chariot soldier
unearthed from Pit No.2

65. Back view of a chariot soldier unearthed
from Pit No.2

66. One hand of a chariot soldier unearthed
from Pit No.2 in a gesture of holding a long
weapon.

67. Feet of a terra-cotta standing chariot
soldier unearthed from Pit No.2

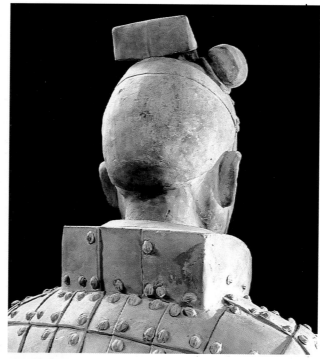

68、御手俑(二號俑坑出土)

69、御手俑的盆領[即頸甲](二號俑坑出土)

70、御手俑的頭部[背視](二號俑坑出土)

71、御手俑的甲衣(二號俑坑出土)

68. A Terra-cotta charioteer unearthed from Pit No.2

69. Armoured gorget of a terra-cotta charioteer unearthed from Pit No.2

70. Back of a charioteer's head from Pit No.2

71. Armoured coat of a terra-cotta charioteer unearthed from Pit No.2

72、袍俑(頭像局部)

73、鎧甲俑(頭像局部)

74、將軍俑(頭像局部)

75、騎兵俑(頭像局部)

76、鎧甲俑的手勢(此俑的手勢特殊,持物不明)

77、鎧甲俑右手持長兵器的手勢

78、將軍俑的手勢,雙手交垂於腹前,作挂劍狀。

79、鎧甲俑的手勢(此俑的手勢特殊,持物不明)

80、立射俑的手勢(二號俑坑出土)

81、御手俑的護手甲(二號俑坑出土)

72. Part of the head of a terra-cotta robed warrior

73. Part of the head of a terra-cotta armoured warrior

74. Part of the head of a terra-cotta general

75. Part of the head of a terra-cotta cavalryman

76. A terra-cotta armoured warrior's hand whose gesture is unique. The object which is held by him is unidentified.

77. Right hand of a terra-cotta armoured warrior, seemingly holding a long weapon

78. A terra-cotta general's hand gesture: He crosses his hands over his abdomen in the gesture of leaning on a sword

79. A terra-cotta armoured warrior's hand whose gesture is unique. The object which is held by him is unidentified.

80. The hand gesture of a terra-cotta standing archer unearthed from Pit No.2

81. A terra-cotta charioteer's gauntlets, unearthed from Pit No.2

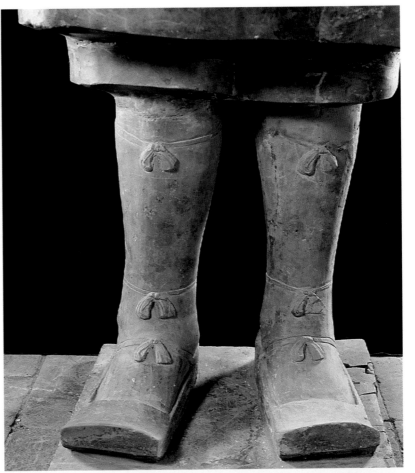

82、立射俑的雙足立姿(二號俑坑出土)

83、行縢：輕裝步兵俑腿部都紮行縢(即裹腿)

84、蹲跪俑的足及履底的花紋

82. Feet of a terra-cotta standing archer, unearthed from Pit No.2

83. Wrappings: Legs of all terra-cotta lightly-equipped infantrymen are lashed with wrappings.

84. Pattern of a terra-cotta kneeling archer's sole

85、將軍俑的甲衣背視
86、軍吏俑［局部］(一號俑坑出土)
87、軍吏俑的頭冠
88、軍吏俑頭戴的長冠

85. A back view of a terra-cotta general's armour
86. Part of a terra-cotta officer unearthed from Pit No.1
87. Cap of a terra-cotta officer
88. A terra-cotta officer's long cap

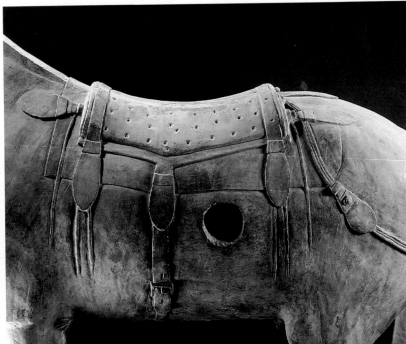

89、陶馬的頭部(二號俑坑出土)
90、拉車馬俑的卷尾(一號俑坑出土)
91、馬身上雕的鞍韉(二號俑坑出土)
92、騎兵鞍馬：身長2米，通首高1.72米，作
　　舉頸嘶鳴狀。馬身上雕着鞍韉、鞦和肚
　　帶、剪鬃、辮尾(二號俑坑出土)
93、騎兵鞍馬的辮尾(二號俑坑出土)

89. Head of a terra-cotta horse unearthed
    from Pit No.2
90. Curved tail of a terra-cotta horse to pull a
    chariot unearthed from Pit No.1
91. Saddle carved on a terra-cotta horse
    unearthed from Pit No.2
92. Cavalryman's saddled horse: It is 2 m. in
    length and 1.72 m. in height, in a posture of
    raising its head and neighing. A saddle,
    harnesses, girth, cut-braistle and plaited
    tail are carved on the horse. Unearthed
    from Pit No.2
93. Plaited tail of a terra-cotta cavalryman's
    saddled horse unearthed from Pit No.2

94、陶俑頭像(一號俑坑出土)

95、陶俑面部殘存的彩繪顏色

94. Head of a terra-cotta warrior unearthed
   from Pit No.1

95. Remnants of colours left on a terra-cotta
   warrior's face

96、陶俑面部残存的彩绘颜色

96. Remnants of colours left on a terra-cotta
    warrior's face

$T_2 : D_1$

97、陶俑面部殘存的彩繪顏色
98、陶俑頭部殘存的彩繪顏色
99、陶俑頭部殘存的彩繪顏色
100、陶俑頭部殘存的彩繪顏色
101、陶俑面部殘存的彩繪顏色
102、陶俑面部殘存的彩繪顏色
103、陶俑身上殘存的彩繪顏色
104、軍吏俑鎧甲上殘存的彩繪顏色

97. Remnants of colours left on a terra-cotta warrior's face
98. Remnants of colours left on a terra-cotta warrior's head
99. Remnants of colours left on a terra-cotta warrior's head
100. Remnants of colours left on a terra-cotta warrior's head
101. Remnants of colours left on a terra-cotta warrior's face
102. Remnants of colours left on a terra-cotta warrior's face
103. Remnants of colours left on a terra-cotta warrior's body
104. Remnants of colours left on armours of a terra-cotta officer

105、青銅劍：長91厘米，劍身最寬處3.65厘米，出土時基本無銹，非常鋒利(一號俑坑出土)。

106、銅鏃一束(一號俑坑出土)

105. Bronze swords: each one is 91cm. in length and 3.63 cm. in its widest width unearthed from Pit No.1

106. Bronze arrowheads unearthed from Pit No.1

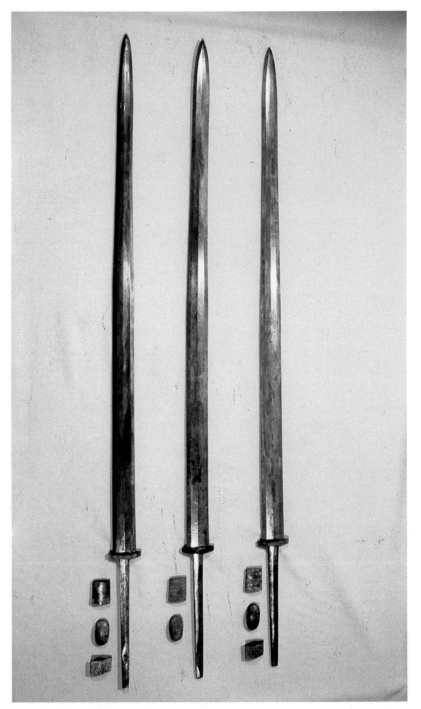

107、銅矛

108、銅弩機(一號俑坑出土)

109、銅殳(三號俑坑出土)

107. Bronze spear heads

108. Bronze triggers unearthed from Pit No.1

109. Bronze SHU (an ancient Chinese weapon)
      unearthed from pit No.3

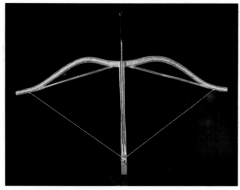

110、弩的複製模型

111、銅戟：爲戈與矛的聯合體(一號俑坑出
土)

110. A reproduction of a crossbow

111. A bronze halberd, a combination of
dagger and spear, unearthed from Pit
No.1

112、蹲跪射俑
113、陶俑群像(一號俑坑出土)

112. A terra-cotta archer in kneeling position
113. Terra-cotta warriors unearthed from Pit
    No.1

114、將軍俑(二號俑坑出土)

115、立身俑(一號俑坑出土)

114. A terra-cotta general unearthed from Pit
No.2

115. A terra-cotta standing warrior unearthed
from Pit No.1

116、袍俑(一號俑坑出土)
117、御手俑(一號俑坑出土)

116. A terra-cotta robed warrior unearthed from Pit No.1
117. A terra-cotta charioteer unearthed from Pit No.1

118、一號兵馬俑坑出土的戰車的四匹陶馬
　　及車前武士俑的隊列

119、將軍俑頭像

118. A chariot pulled by four terra-cotta horses
　　in front of which are terra-cotta warriors,
　　unearthed from Pit No.1

119. Head of a terra-cotta general unearthed
　　from Pit No.1

120、軍吏俑頭像：他頭戴長冠，冠上有帶繫
　　結頷下，帶尾飄拂胸前（一號俑坑出
　　土）。

121、 袍俑頭像（一號俑坑出土）

122、 袍俑頭像（一號俑坑出土）

120. Head of a terra-cotta officer: He wears a
long cap whose laces are tied under his
chin and their ends flutter above his chest.
Unearthed from Pit No.1

121. Head of a terra-cotta robed warrior
unearthed from Pit No.1

122. Head of a terra-cotta robed warrior
unearthed from Pit No.1

123、鎧甲俑頭像(一號俑坑出土)
124、御手俑側面像

123. Head of a terra-cotta armoured warrior
unearthed from Pit No.1
124. A profile of a terra-cotta charioteer

125、立射俑頭像(二號俑坑出土)

126、軍吏俑(一號俑坑出土)

127、御手俑(一號俑坑出土)

125. Head of a terra-cotta standing archer unearthed from Pit No. 2

126. A terra-cotta officer unearthed from Pit No. 1

127. A terra-cotta charioteer unearthed from Pit No. 1

128、 車士俑(一號俑坑出土)

129、 御手俑(一號俑坑出土)

128. A terra-cotta chariot soldier unearthed
from Pit No.1

129. A terra-cotta charioteer unearthed from
Pit No.1

130、鎧甲俑(一號俑坑出土)

131、鎧甲俑(一號俑坑出土)

130. A terra-cotta armoured warrior unearthed from Pit No.1

131. A terra-cotta armoured warrior unearthed from Pit No.1

132、鎧甲俑(一號俑坑出土)
133、鎧甲俑(一號俑坑出土)
134、鎧甲俑(一號俑坑出土)
135、鎧甲俑(一號俑坑出土)

132. A terra-cotta armoured warrior unearthed from Pit No.1
133. A terra-cotta armoured warrior unearthed from Pit No.1
134. A terra-cotta armoured warrior unearthed from Pit No.1
135. A terra-cotta armoured warrior unearthed from Pit No.1

136、鎧甲俑(一號俑坑出土)

137、鎧甲俑(一號俑坑出土)

136. A terra-cotta armoured warrior unearthed from Pit No.1

137. A terra-cotta armoured warrior unearthed from Pit No.1

138、袍俑(一號俑坑出土)
139、袍俑(一號俑坑出土)
140、袍俑(一號俑坑出土)

138. A terra-cotta robed warrior unearthed from Pit No.1
139. A terra-cotta robed warrior unearthed from Pit No.1
140. A terra-cotta robed warrior unearthed from Pit No.1

141、袍俑(一號俑坑出土)

142、袍俑(一號俑坑出土)

141. A terra-cotta robed warrior unearthed
from Pit No.1

142. A terra-cotta robed warrior unearthed
from Pit No.1

143、袍俑(一號俑坑出土)

144、袍俑(一號俑坑出土)

145、袍俑(一號俑坑出土)

146、袍俑(一號俑坑出土)

147、袍俑(一號俑坑出土)

148、袍俑(一號俑坑出土)

149、袍俑(一號俑坑出土)

143. A terra-cotta robed warrior unearthed
    from Pit No.1

144. A terra-cotta robed warrior unearthed
    from Pit No.1

145. A terra-cotta robed warrior unearthed
    from Pit No.1

146. A terra-cotta robed warrior unearthed
    from Pit No.1

147. A terra-cotta robed warrior unearthed
    from Pit No.1

148. A terra-cotta robed warrior unearthed
    from Pit No.1

149. A terra-cotta robed warrior unearthed
    from Pit No.1

150、陶俑髮式(一號俑坑出土)

151、鎧甲俑腦後的扁髻(一號俑坑出土)

150. Hair style of a terra-cotta warrior unearthed from Pit No.1

151. A flat bun on the back of the head of a terra-cotta armoured warrior unearthed from Pit No.1

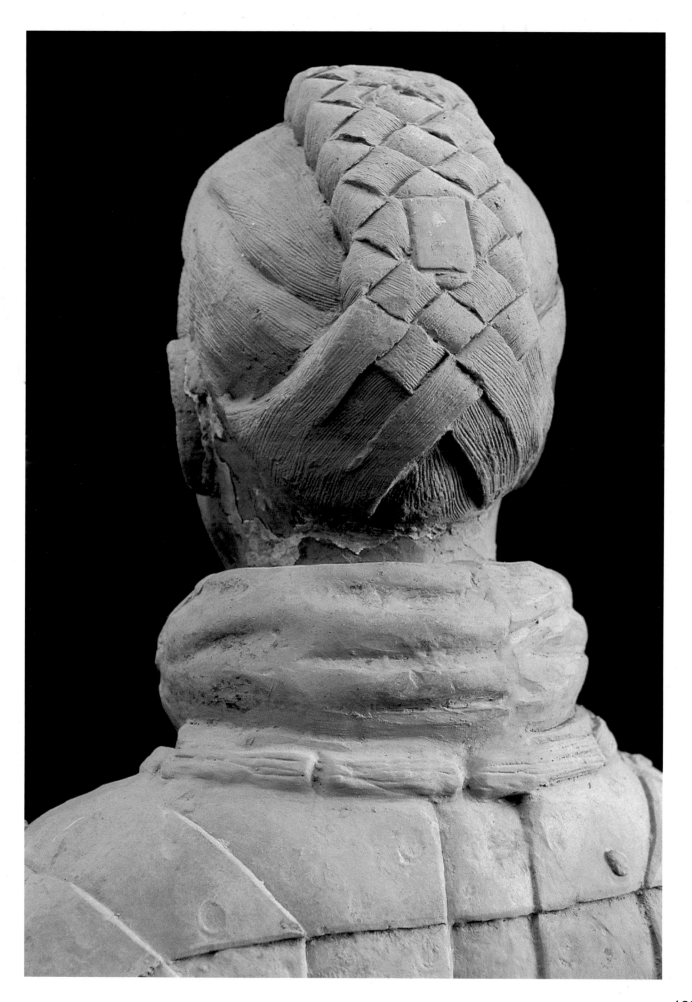

152、鎧甲俑腦後的扁髻(一號俑坑出土)
153、陶俑髮式(一號俑坑出土)
154、陶俑髮式(一號俑坑出土)
155、陶俑髮式(一號俑坑出土)
156、陶俑髮式(一號俑坑出土)
157、軍吏俑的髮型和冠(一號俑坑出土)
158、陶俑的髮式(一號俑坑出土)

152. A flat bun of a terra-cotta armoured warrior unearthed from Pit No.1
153. Hair style of a terra-cotta warrior unearthed from Pit No.1
154. Hair style of a terra-cotta warrior unearthed from Pit No.1
155. Hair style of a terra-cotta warrior unearthed from Pit No.1
156. Hair style of a terra-cotta warrior unearthed from Pit No.1
157. Hair style and cap of terra-cotta officers from Pit No.1
158. Hair style of a terra-cotta warrior unearthed from Pit No.1

159、一號兵馬俑坑軍陣的東南角
160、 觀衆在欣賞這一列列、一行行排列有
　　 序的兵馬俑。

159. The southeast corner of the battle
　　 formation in Pit No.1
160. Visitors admiring the well-ranked terra-
　　 cotta army

161、袁仲一先生
162、羅忠民先生

161. Mr. Yuan Zhongyi
162. Mr. Luo Zhongmin

編 后 話

　　本《畫册》撰文者，是袁仲一先生。1963年，他畢業于華東師範大學中國古代史研究生班。　1964年至今，一直在陝西省考古研究所和秦始皇兵馬俑博物館工作。現任秦始皇兵馬俑博物館館長，陝西省考古研究所副所長、研究員、華東師範大學中國古文化研究中心兼職教授，陝西省考古學會副會長。

　　袁仲一主要從事秦漢考古和中國古文字的研究。自1974年秦始皇陵兵馬俑坑發現後至今的15年間，一直主持和親自參與秦始皇陵園的勘探和兵馬俑坑的發掘及研究工作，獲得了豐碩的考古成果。在研究工作方面，公開發表論文70余篇，以及專著、編著、圖錄八部，共170余萬言。其代表作有：《秦始皇陵兵馬俑坑——一號坑發掘報告》（1974年－1984年），《秦始皇陵兵馬俑》、《秦陵二號銅車馬》、《秦代陶文》等著作。

　　本《畫册》主要攝影者，是著名文物攝影家羅忠民先生。他自1954年即從事專職文物攝影工作。三十多年，他風風雨雨地走遍了陝西省的所有考古工地。

　　1974年，他受命加入了陝西省秦始皇陵兵馬俑考古隊的行列。多年來的創作實踐，使他運用攝影藝術造型的技巧，達到了爐火純青的境界。他的每一幅攝影作品，都能作到內容和形式的和諧統一，構圖簡單明快而含蘊深豐，令人遠看一目了然；近看則品味無窮，既可供藝術欣賞，又可供科學研究。他所拍攝的秦兵馬俑，既在總體上保持了原有的面貌，又在個體上表現得纖毫畢露，精神煥發。讀者欣賞時，有如身臨其境。

Editor's Note

　　Mr. Yuan Zhongyi, the writer of this picture album, graduated in 1963 from a postgraduate class studying China's ancient history at the Huadong Normal University. From 1964 until now, he has been working at the Shaanxi Provincial Archaeological Research Institute and the Museum of Emperor Qin Shi Huang's Terra-cotta Warriors and Horses. Now he is the director of the Museum, vice president of the Shaanxi Archaeological Research Institute, research fellow, concurrently professor of the research centre of China's ancient culture at the Huadong Normal University, and vice president of the Shaanxi Provincial Archaeological Society.

　　Yuan Zhongyi mainly engages in research of archaeology of the Qin and Han dynasties and ancient Chinese characters. In the last 15 years since the discovery of the Qin terra-cotta army, he has been in charge of, and participated in as well, the survey of the necropolis of Emperor Qin Shi Huang and the excavation and study of the terra-cotta army that have resulted in rich archaeological achievements. In research work, he has published over 70 essays, and 8 monographs, compilations and catalogues, totalling more than 1.7 million Chinese characters. His representative works include "A Report on the Excavation of the Terra-cotta Army Pit No.1", "The Terra-cotta Army at the Mausoleum of Emperor Qin Shi Huang", "No.2 Bronze Chariot and Horses at the Qin Mausoleum" and "Inscriptions Borne on Potteries of the Qin Dynasty", etc.

　　Mr. Luo Zhongmin, the main photographer of this picture album, is a famous photographer of cultural relics. In the last more than 30 years since he started to work as a professional photographer on cultural relics in 1954, he travelled to all archaeological sites of Shaanxi province in spite of winds and rains. In 1974, he was asked to participate in the archaeological team of the terra-cotta army at Emperor Qin Shi Huang's Mausoleum of Shaanxi Province. Years of creative practice have brought his skill in photographic art to a high perfection. Each of his photographic works is in perfect harmony in both content and form. Its composition is simple, lively, and meaningful, perfectly clear at first sight from afar, and it is pregnant with rich meaning at close sight. His works are for artistic appreciation as well as for scientific research. In his photographs, the Qin terra-cotta figures generally keep their original features, and individually present viewers with striking details, making them feel personally on the scene.